**The Micr**

| The time: | the very near future |
| The characters: | Thor Benson, a fifteen-year-old computer whizz-kid |
| | Kevin and Pamela Powell, his neighbours and friends. |

They comprise the MicroKidz and, together with their high-tech computer know-how and Mr Chips, Thor's ingenious robot, they're heading for mystery and adventure.

*Fission Chips* is the third MicroKidz mystery.

**Also by the same author,
and available in Knight Books:**

The Cagey Bee Byte
Computer Mind Games
Data Snatchers

THE MICROKIDZ MYSTERY ADVENTURES · THE MICROKIDZ MYSTERY ADVENTURES · THE MICROKIDZ MYSTERY ADVENTURES · THE MICROKIDZ MYSTERY ADVENTURES · THE MICROKIDZ MYSTERY ADVENTURES · THE MICROKIDZ MYSTERY ADVENTURES

# THE MICROKIDZ MYSTERY ADVENTURES

# Fission Chips

## G. P. JORDAN

KNIGHT BOOKS
Hodder and Stoughton

Copyright © 1984 by G. P. Jordan
First published in Canada by General Paperbacks 1984
*First published in Great Britain by Knight Books 1985*

**British Library C.I.P.**

Jordan, G. P.
  Fission chips.—(The MicroKidz mystery
  adventures)
  I. Title  II. Series
  813′.54[J]      PZ7

ISBN 0–340–37181–1

*The characters and situations in this book are
entirely imaginary and bear no relation to any real
person or actual happening*

This book is sold subject to the condition that
it shall not, by way of trade or otherwise, be
lent, re-sold, hired out or otherwise circulated
without the publisher's prior consent in any
form of binding or cover other than that in
which it is published and without a similar
condition including this condition being
imposed on the subsequent purchaser.

Printed and bound in Great Britain for
Hodder and Stoughton Paperbacks, a
division of Hodder and Stoughton Ltd.,
Mill Road, Dunton Green, Sevenoaks
Kent (Editorial Office: 47 Bedford
Square, London, WC1 3DP) by
Richard Clay (The Chaucer Press) Ltd.,
Bungay, Suffolk

# CHAPTER 1
# Reactor, Reactions

"Old nuclear reactors never die. And they won't fade away."

"Why not?"

Edward Benson looked at his son sitting next to him in the passenger seat of the family car. Thor's seemingly simple question really required a long explanation, but a basic answer would have to do for now.

"Because the 'fading away' takes thousands of years," the man stated calmly. "The half-life deterioration rate of some fission byproducts is thirty years. But once they have been radioactive, the danger never leaves."

Thor Benson contemplated this fact. His dark blue eyes reflected his concern. At fifteen years of age, Thor realized that the world was much more complex than he had once believed.

"How can we be sure, Dad?"

"Like many other things in life, it's a matter of faith," replied Mr. Benson. "We trust in our scientists and their work. We have to believe what they tell us."

"But thousands of years?" came the voice of Kevin Powell from the back seat. "I can't wait that long."

Thor looked around at the heavier youth who was a year older than himself. His best friend was a kidder, often using wisecracks to cover up his own fears.

"What's wrong, Kevin? Don't want to talk about nuclear power?"

"Not before lunch," he answered quickly.

"Maybe you'll be able to combine them," Edward Benson said, as he pointed ahead to their destination. "That is if the cafeteria is still open."

Kevin got another joke in. "I always wanted to try uranium-fried chicken!"

On the horizon they could see the twin cooling towers of the Emerald Nuclear Generating Station. These solid concrete reactor buildings cast a dark shadow on the surrounding landscape. Once they had powered industries, heated homes, and lighted nearby cities. Now these same towers stood unused, exhausted by time and radioactivity.

"They don't look any different," murmured Thor.

"Not from out here," replied his father. "But they're useless now, like candles left standing after the wick has burned out."

Edward drove up to the entrance. Strict security measures remained in effect. A guard took Mr. Benson's identification pass, scanned it through a portable Q-D-Tector and waited. A green crystal flashed on top of the device.

"Thank you, sir," the guard said as he handed the card back. "Parking is available near the main building."

The car lurched forward into the compound. Thor turned around as Kevin lowered the rear window.

"Remember our promise?"

Kevin nodded his head slowly. He had been briefed on proper conduct, once by Mr. Benson and again by Thor. Since the trip was conditional on his agreeing to their promise, he went along with it. Still, Kevin wondered, what could be wrong with requesting a special souvenir?

"All right, boys. This is it."

The car pulled into the visitors' parking lot. Edward flipped off his seatbelt, checked the recharge timer, and climbed out. With Thor and Kevin following behind him, he walked into the main office building.

"What a difference a year makes," muttered Mr. Benson.

Workmen were scuttling across the dusty foyer. Where flowers had once bloomed and ferns prospered, there remained only empty boxes. Mounds of garbage replaced sleek office desks and plush carpeting. The building had been transformed into a warehouse of waste.

Stepping around a pile of discarded furniture, Mr. Benson led the youths toward an elevator. Two technicians were already on board. These men ignored the visitors and continued chattering.

"I'm fed up with driving out to that place. This will be the third time today," said the tall, reedlike man.

"What can you do?" his small, balding friend said. "Orders are orders."

"Triple Pyramids is backed up. Why do they need more?"

"Not for car parts, that's for sure," laughed the bald man.

Both technicians got off at the third floor. They left three bewildered passengers in the elevator.

"Sounds as if someone isn't happy with his job," said Thor.

"Nothing new in that," replied Edward. "To keep everyone working and happy is nearly impossible."

Kevin, meanwhile, had found something of interest. He reached down into the corner of the elevator.

"They forgot this," he said, lifting a brown cylinder casing.

Mr. Benson examined it.

"So you still managed to collect a souvenir," Thor joked.

"We'll stop back at that floor on the way out," Mr.

Benson told them. "It should be easy enough to find those men and return this."

A bell rang as their stop came up. Master Control was the topmost level in the building. The doors slid open and the visitors emerged.

No one was present to greet them. The area was empty of all personnel. Equipment and electronics gear lay strewn about on the floor, as if plundered by a horde of animals.

"What a mess!" exclaimed Thor.

They stepped carefully into the middle of the huge room. A vacant observation deck along the upper walls bordered the area. Hundreds of tourists daily had once walked along its pathway to watch the controllers who ordered up nuclear power and relayed it to homes and factories. Now, shattered glass filled that observation path.

Edward Benson strode over to the central communications desk. He cleared a layer of dust from the front panel. An array of switches and buttons became evident. Absent-mindedly, he ran his hand across them.

"I helped install these," he whispered.

The youngsters looked at the older man in silent respect.

"It was my first big job after graduating," he continued, studying the scene. "Did you know I worked in this room before you were both born?"

The pair nodded.

"And what's left standing?" cracked Kevin.

"The people," smiled Edward.

"You feel kind of homesick here, Dad?"

"Seventeen years is a long time. When I helped set up the data processing and computer systems in this place, we were pioneers. One of the first. Engineers and designers of other nuclear generating stations came from all over the world to study our assembly."

"And now the disassembly."

"Decommissioning," Mr. Benson corrected. "That's the proper term."

He led the two boys over to a sealed door. Its hinges appeared welded to the frame. A digital lock on the handle hung loose.

"This was our emergency bunker," he chuckled. "In case of a major spill or accident we were supposed to take refuge in here."

"Was it ever used?" asked Kevin.

"Only on lunch breaks. Otherwise, it was our last resort. Thank goodness we didn't have to find out if it really was effective."

A man came into view on the top observation deck. His helmet and sash identified him as a security guard.

"This area is off-limits!" he declared.

"I'm here to see Professor Coleman," replied Edward. "We have an appointment."

"Would you mind returning to the ground floor then?"

Kevin and Thor shrugged at each other. With the generating plant inactive, it hardly seemed necessary to enforce the security rules. Still, they had to comply.

The youths followed Mr. Benson to the elevator. Just as they entered, Kevin remembered his discovery.

"Hold on a minute," he said, dashing back into the control room.

He had placed the cylinder casing against a switching panel. He picked it up and started back to the waiting elevator.

"Stop right there!"

The shout thundered throughout the room. Kevin froze in his tracks. The security guard was pointing a gun!

"Put that back!" he ordered.

Kevin dropped the casing, and its metal contents struck the floor with a clatter.

"Hey, relax!" shouted Mr. Benson. He stepped back into the room with Thor.

"No stealing!" shouted the guard.

"The boy brought that here. He found it in the elevator and was going to return it!" Edward was getting angry. He hated seeing someone falsely accused. To make matters worse, Kevin was being challenged by an armed guard.

The guard moved down the ramp and approached the trio.

"You should apologize," said Mr. Benson.

The guard smirked. His short hair, cropped so tight it bristled like a brush, framed his stern face. A name tag carried his identity, "Douglas Mills." With his free arm, Mills retrieved the cylinder casing.

"Let's take a ride downstairs to get better acquainted," he sneered.

They stepped into the elevator. The tension rose as they descended. When the light indicating Level Three came on, Kevin made a suggestion.

"That's where the men who left this went. Why don't we see them?"

Douglas Mills didn't reply.

Edward Benson refrained from speaking out. A better opportunity would occur soon, he hoped.

When they reached the ground floor, the guard got out first. He directed the visitors toward a hallway that ran the length of the building. Edward knew the area well.

"If we are going anywhere, it is to see Professor Coleman," he stated. "I have his authorization to be here."

The guard whispered inside an open door. A brightly lit room with several workers was beyond. One technician stepped out. It was the small balding man from the elevator.

"What's that doing here?" he snapped upon seeing the cylinder.

"He had it," Mills said, pointing at Kevin.

The technician shot a cold glance at the boy, grabbed the brown casing, and scurried from the area.

"What's the problem?"

The visitors turned to face a tall, thin man in the hallway. His white helmet read Project Supervisor.

"This hotshot guard is the problem!" Edward Benson railed. "We were in the Master Control room. My son's friend found that article and was returning it to your technician when this guard drew his weapon!"

"Is that correct, Doug?"

"Yes," came the reply. "This boy took a cylinder from a restricted zone."

"But it was already . . ."

Kevin was cut off. The project supervisor raised his hand for silence. Mr. Benson's patience was at an end.

"If you will direct us to Professor Alan Coleman, we can settle this very quickly."

The supervisor reacted rudely. "You're out of luck there, mister. Coleman's gone."

"But he couldn't be," Edward insisted. "I spoke to him yesterday. We had an appointment for this very hour!"

The news did not interest the man. He suggested they leave the building at once.

"And who is ordering us?"

"I am! Ray Ginsler!"

A heated exchange between Mr. Benson and the supervisor followed. The two boys feared it might come to blows. The fact that Edward was one of the original data control designers soon settled the matter.

"Why didn't you say that first?" Ray Ginsler asked.

Edward shook his head. "Why? Would your guard not have pulled out his weapon?"

Ray shifted his white hard hat onto the back of his head. Doug Mills was leaning against the wall. The supervisor motioned for the guard to depart.

"Okay, Doug, I have it now," Ginsler said coolly.

When Mills had left them, Ginsler steered the group to his office. The boys made their way toward his expansive window. It had a view of the entire area. Mr. Benson took a seat opposite Ray Ginsler.

"Try getting Al Coleman," the supervisor barked into an intercom. Then he turned his face to Edward. "So you're one of the original Emerald Nukers, huh?"

"My responsibilities were only in the communications branch," Benson clarified. "All the nuclear assembly control came under Professor Coleman."

That point required no explanation. Ginsler knew the roles in that department. His interests were more precise. He waved at the work in progress outside, at the trucks and heavy machinery rumbling across the property.

"I bet when you folks built this place you thought it was going to last forever."

Mr. Benson nodded slowly, wondering what the man was getting at.

"So what does it feel like seeing your dream, your prized project, being torn down?"

Edward shifted in his seat. The tone of the question made him uncomfortable. He was spared having to answer when the desk intercom interrupted them.

"Mr. Coleman just returned your call, sir," reported the secretary. "Said he forgot the meeting with Mr. Benson and is driving back at once."

Now that Edward Benson's story had been verified, both men could relax. Ray Ginsler smiled at Edward across the desk and leaned back in his chair. Mr. Benson turned his attention back to the boys.

Thor and Kevin were fascinated with the work going on outside. Huge cranes were raising steel girders around the rear of the twin towers. Scaffolds reached halfway up one tower. Trucks deposited soil for bulldozers to spread across a field. Men in forklift vehicles shifted loads under the direction of foremen.

"Why don't you boys go out and take a closer look at all that?" Ray suggested.

"I'd prefer they stay indoors," countered Edward.

"Heck, they know enough to be careful. Besides, the professor won't be here for a bit. Maybe you can tell me some things about the construction of old Emerald."

There seemed no sense in subjecting the youths once more to such a conversation, Mr. Benson realized. In fact, he'd prefer not to participate himself. However, since this man Ginsler was an associate of his former employer, it would be impolite to refuse.

"Don't wander far," he finally said.

The boys gladly left the room. They were feeling uncomfortable in the strained atmosphere of the facility. The fresh air came as a welcome relief.

"Thought I was going to choke in there," Thor said.

"And I felt like choking that guy in there," Kevin added crossly. "Talk about rude treatment. Guns pointed. Smart-aleck supervisors. You'd think we were in the army!"

"You joker!" laughed Thor. "Didn't I warn you when we first got here? No souvenirs! And look what happens. You find one anyway!"

"But that was chance, an accident," pleaded Kevin. "You saw for yourself. It wasn't my fault."

"Kevin, is it ever?"

Kevin and Thor were used to sharing jokes together.

They had grown up across the street from each other and were best friends. Along with Kevin's sister Pamela, who was the same age as Thor, they had faced the challenges of the adventures that had come their way. Solving mysteries that involved microsystems and high-tech problems had earned the youngsters a growing reputation. The national press had dubbed the trio "The MicroKidz." A recent case, *MIND GAMES,* had ended in the arrest of scientists seeking to control the brainwaves of youngsters around the country. These villains had disguised their method by using rigged interactive video games to steal the thoughts of unsuspecting players. Special action by Thor and Pamela had saved the minds of Kevin Powell and millions of other youngsters.

"It could have been worse," Kevin stated.

"Right. So the next time you see something like that cylinder casing, leave it alone," Thor told him. "Remember what curiosity did to the cat."

"I'd rather think what it did for Einstein."

A huge crane swung across the sky. Dangling from its end was a steel girder. The entire area was blanketed by the loud drone of heavy machinery.

"Check that action!" Thor shouted above the noise.

He pointed to a crew of workers on the top rim of a reactor tower. They were dwarfed by the immense structure. Each man was pulling at a steel cable. As the lines were dropped down the exterior of the tower, one of the men suddenly lost his grip, slipped, and fell.

"Look out!" Thor screamed.

His voice was lost in the clamor of activity.

Kevin began to walk backwards while staring at the accident sight. The panic among the reactor crew was evident. As their fellow worker clung desperately to the swinging cable, they shouted for help.

Thor turned to see what Kevin was doing and caught sight of a large object off to one side. It seemed to be moving toward them. As he watched, he realized that the object was gaining speed and definitely heading in their direction. A dump truck was rushing out of control. And Kevin Powell, deafened by all the noise, was backing directly into its path!

# CHAPTER 2

# Salvaging Past Treasures

Thor Benson had no time to panic, he had to act swiftly. The truck was speeding closer every nanosecond and Kevin wouldn't hear him shout a warning.

With a football-like sprint, Thor charged into Kevin and drove the heavier youth backwards, out of the truck's way. The tackle ended against a parked car.

Before Kevin even had a chance to yell, the huge dump truck roared past, barely an arm's length away! He knew then that his life had been saved.

"What? Who's that driver?" he shivered.

They caught sight of a peculiar marking on the truck's mudflaps: three white pyramids. The image burned itself into their memories.

"Help! Help!"

The youths saw the terrified worker still hanging from the reactor cooling tower. His cable swung from side to side, each motion bringing him closer to death.

The constant heavy equipment noise blocked out the crew's pleas. Many ground workers wore enclosed hard hat helmets with ear protectors. They went about their duties oblivious to the unfolding drama.

"Come on Thor, inside!"

It was Kevin's turn to be heroic. He ran into the main office complex, past the vacant reception desks, and toward the project supervisor's area.

Thor reached the doorway moments later. His father and Ray Ginsler were already at the window. Kevin was pointing to the reactor tower.

"How long can that cable hold him?"

"The real question is how long can he hold onto the cable," Ray said to Edward. He spun about, reached for the intercom, and pressed the Emergency Alert switch. "Rescue units to Tower One! Extension ladders and ambulance!"

The trio pursued Ginsler through the private doorway which was his disguised entrance. Work halted around the site. The alarm system blared unceasingly. Sirens preceded the arrival of the Emergency Squad.

"Stay with me, boys," ordered Mr. Benson. "No getting in the way of things!"

Kevin and Thor glanced knowingly at each other. Both were thankful Mr. Benson was unaware of their own near-accident. He would surely have taken them home at once.

The rescue of the stranded worker commenced. The Emergency Squad was well-drilled, its tactics precise and sure. An extension ladder zoomed up the side of the reactor tower. Two men in its cage reached for the clinging worker.

Suddenly the swinging cable snapped!

Everyone gasped. Then, one group of workers after another began to applaud. The stranded crewman had fallen safely into the rescue cage.

"That saves his bacon!" barked Ray Ginsler at a nearby foreman. "I want a full report this afternoon!"

The project supervisor brushed past the gathering and made for the tower. The rest took this as a cue to resume their work. Heavy equipment sounds started up once more. The safety cage was retracted, bringing the shaken crewman to the ground. He was assisted into a rescue vehicle and driven away.

Edward Benson patted his son's shoulder. Together with Kevin Powell, they watched the decommission process resume.

"The Emerald Nuclear Generating Station is going to be only a memory in six months," he told the pair. "Take a good look at it, fellows, because it won't be standing much longer."

"Are they going to tear down those towers?" Kevin wondered.

"They'll be the last to go. First, the fuel rods bundled in the reactor core have to be removed. That's happening now."

"Is it dangerous?"

"Not really. The radioactive pellets inside the fuel rods are transferred in special cases. They would only be a hazard if they were misplaced."

A tractor-trailer truck bearing a Danger: Radioactive Materials sign rumbled slowly past. It followed a circuit that led to a loading ramp at the side of reactor Tower One. A group of men dressed in protective clothing wheeled a cart onto the ramp.

"That might be some spent fuel rods," guessed Mr. Benson.

They watched the shippers load the contents into the rear of the tractor-trailer. Their self-assurance in handling the dangerous cargo was mildly comforting.

While Mr. Benson continued to point out other matters of interest, a green vehicle drove into the parking lot. The elderly man at the wheel tapped the horn and waved. Edward responded to the greeting.

"Professor Alan Coleman," he said soon after, introducing the gentleman to the boys.

"Ah, yes. I've heard about you lads," the professor nodded. "And isn't there another? A girl?"

"Pamela," explained Thor. "She's Kevin's sister. But she had to work today."

"Two out of three MicroKidz isn't bad," chuckled the professor. "Your father is proud of your achievements."

"He keeps that a secret from us," Thor kidded.

Mr. Benson gave his son a playful punch on the shoulder as the professor indicated that they follow along. Acquaintances were renewed as they walked toward the main office building. Although the two men had kept in touch by VistaPhone and by exchanging CompuNews, it had been years since they'd shaken hands in person.

Thor watched the older man lead them into the foyer. The difference in age mattered little here. Professor Coleman, though he was probably a grandfather, and maybe even a great-grandfather, moved swiftly. He had the brisk reflexes of one who has kept himself fit. His mane of grey hair and his drooping white moustache reminded the boy of a famous old poet.

They took the elevator to the Master Control room. They encountered no security guards this time, and Mr. Benson had apparently decided not to report the earlier incident.

"Ah, we had some times in here," laughed the elderly man. "Remember the first big crisis at Emerald?"

Edward shook his head, unable to recall.

"I'll give you a hint. It was the toilet."

Mr. Benson remembered now and chuckled. The boys wondered aloud what it might be.

The professor told them, happy to recount an incident

that had really occurred. "This nuclear plant had been on-line only a few hours. The reactor was running smoothly at 1,500,000 watts. Then someone flushed a toilet. That reduced the main water pressure. It triggered a safety device, and the next moment the entire system shut down! Three days went by before we made the connection."

They all laughed at the funny story. Mr. Benson admitted knowing who was responsible, but wouldn't name him.

"Those were the days," smiled Edward. "Everything seemed possible. We didn't know quite what we were doing, so trial and error became an honorable scientific method."

"And I'm sure you lads have learned from our mistakes," the professor said. He took Mr. Benson by the arm and directed him to the communication racks. "I imagine this is what most interests you. And them."

Even though the years of constant operation had taken their toll on the material, much of it was still usable. Mr. Benson had requested the opportunity to salvage some parts. Since Edward had worked on the design and installation of the data system, the professor had agreed wholeheartedly.

"Take whatever you need, fellows. The rest is only going to be dumped."

For Kevin Powell and Thor Benson it was an incredible invitation. They felt like kids in a candy factory. Whatever they could extract and pile onto a flatbed trolley cart was theirs!

"Anything at all?" they checked again.

The professor took a seat beside the switching panel and watched them. Under Mr. Benson's guidance, the two youths began to dismantle important sections. Some of the microsystems were clearly out of date and needed modifications.

"You are correct about that," said Professor Coleman. "That's why we're junking everything. This technology is as obsolete as those reactor towers outside."

"The boys can always use more learning devices," assured Edward.

He had helped his son build an electronics workshop behind the garage. Many of Thor's finest inventions were devised there by updating old equipment for new purposes. Kevin and Pamela Powell joined in those developments. It was more than a hobby to the youngsters.

"Got enough yet?" chuckled the older man.

Three hours passed. Professor Coleman and Edward entertained each other with stories of the past and news of recent events. Occasionally, they stopped to point out vital pieces of equipment. The boys scored on a major discovery deep inside the computer memory storage bank. Kevin emerged, holding a crystalline case. Suspended inside was a ruby-coated metal.

"Amazing!" exclaimed the professor. "I was certain that would have melted down!"

"Is it in the clear?" Edward asked in a concerned voice.

"Oh, certainly," assured the professor. "If we can still see it, then it has to be safe."

Thor held the object up to the light. "What is it?"

"One of the first of its kind," replied the old man. "Though you are perhaps more familiar with the newer, microminiature version. This is a Fission Tracer."

This was a high point, the youths realized. They knew that developments in the nuclear industry had once paralleled discoveries in microtechnology. Each field influenced the other. This Fission Tracer had received pulse codes from the reactor core, registered and interpreted the fission process, and kept track of the decay rates. It was a basic early warning system.

"You might have one problem with it, though," the professor added in a tone of caution.

The youths and Edward awaited the advice.

"It needs a stream of radioactive emissions to be of any use."

"Thanks, professor, but that's a bit too dangerous for us," Thor answered. The youth considered his ability to modify other peculiar pieces of outdated technology. "But I'll tell you, sir. If there is another use for this Fission Tracer, we'll find it!"

"I second that," added Kevin.

They placed the crystalline case with its ruby-coated metal contents onto the cart. Altogether, they had salvaged fifty individual components. Peripheral units abounded. It was a most successful venture.

"If you can't pack that all into your father's car, I'll take the overflow and follow you home."

"That's a wonderful idea, professor. I know that Laraine would love to see you," Edward replied, speaking of his wife.

They trundled the equipment cart into the elevator. Thor and Kevin stood at the front section, while the two men went to the rear. Their descent halted at the third floor. When the door rolled open, two familiar people were waiting to get on. The technicians stepped in, still chattering to each other.

"Was your cylinder all right?" Kevin asked.

The tall, thin man and his bald associate stared at the boy. They were surprised at meeting this same group.

"Yes it was, thank you," mumbled the tall technician.

"You caused us a bit of trouble," Edward told them. "A misunderstanding you should have cleared up."

The technicians appeared embarrassed. The bald man replied.

"We were in a rush, really pressed for time."

When the door opened, they both hurried away.

After the trolley cart had been wheeled through the desolate foyer and out to the parking lot, Professor Coleman asked what had happened. Edward described the encounter briefly.

"Tell me, Kevin," queried the professor. "What did that cylinder weigh?"

"Oh...maybe as much as a watermelon."

Thor laughed to himself. Food was always close to Kevin's thoughts.

"What do you think of that?" the professor asked Edward. "Misplacing a nuclear fuel rod in an elevator!"

"You must know who those men are," Edward inquired. "They're systems personnel."

"I know very little of what is going on at Emerald these days. It's an entirely different place. Construction procedures and control checks are things of the past," the man added. "These decommission specialists are an odd breed."

It took half an hour of creative packing to load the Benson car. However, an assortment of pieces still remained outside. The earlier offer from the professor was accepted.

"Let me check in with Mr. Ginsler before we leave. I don't know when I'll be back on site."

They watched the elderly man return to the building. It gave them time to plan the journey home. The coastal route which had brought them here was fine for leisurely sightseeing, but it was not the quickest way back to Stanton. Mr. Benson decided on the triple expressway transfer.

"One of you should go along with the professor as a navigator. Decide that yourselves."

While Mr. Benson tucked the remaining gear into his car, the boys strolled away. They wanted a last minute look at the reactor cooling towers. It also gave them the chance to decide who should accompany the professor.

"There go your grateful friends," Thor said, pointing to the pair of technicians who had misplaced the fuel rod cylinder casing. The bald man was leading his tall friend to one of the parked trucks. By their animated movements, it appeared that an argument was underway. The bald man took a swipe at the other's back. The blow nearly caused the tall man to topple over.

"Wonder what that's all about?" Kevin mused.

"The guy probably forgot something else!"

The youngsters laughed while they watched the two technicians make for the loading ramp. Scattered there on a platform, awaiting shipment, were dozens of similar brown casings.

"What are they after?" wondered the boys.

The men seemed to find what they wanted after sorting through the pile. The bald man lugged the steel cylinder to the side of the loading ramp. His strained effort indicated that the cylinder was heavy. Then the tall man helped him drag it toward a pickup truck. They tossed it into the rear section of the truck, causing it to sag. Once they had shut the rear gate, the two technicians climbed into the truck's cabin.

"Nothing like a do-it-yourself operation," commented Thor. "At least you can be sure things are done the way you want them."

They turned their attention back to admiring what was left of the mighty generating plant. That Mr. Benson had a connection with its history made their visit increasingly relevant. Now that they had obtained parts of the data system which had once monitored the nuclear plant, the youths had an extra reason to enjoy this final moment at the famous site.

"I know how to solve our return trip problem," Kevin said, after a short while. "Since I have my license, I'll drive the professor's car. He and your Dad can talk some more, and you and I can stick together."

Thor turned to his friend and smiled. "You genius."

They headed back to the parking lot. Mr. Benson had finished packing all the gear and was leaning beside his car. Thor was about to tell him of the new driving plan, when, suddenly, a tremendous boom shook the area.

Sirens wailed. At once, the area filled with frightened workers, their faces showing the dread they felt. Another blast had occurred!

"Thor! Kevin!" shouted Mr. Benson over the panic.

The boys scampered toward him. Old Professor Coleman was also racing from the office building. He shouted to the visitors.

"Fast! It's an alert!"

"Give me your keys, professor!" Kevin shouted.

The man responded automatically. He tossed them at the youth. Before the professor realized what was happening, Kevin was behind the wheel of his car. Thor jumped into the passenger seat, Kevin started the car, shifted into gear, and took off.

Mr. Benson and Professor Coleman were right behind them. The Alert siren sent many workers dashing for their vehicles. Everyone was intent on getting out as quickly as they could.

Kevin swerved to avoid a pickup truck that shot out in front. Its load shifted wildly, forcing the driver into the opposite lane.

Thor caught sight of the two odd technicians in the cabin. A silent alarm went off in his mind when he recognized the design on their truck's mudflaps.

The white triple pyramids!

# CHAPTER 3

# Visit to a Wasteland

The boys lost sight of the veering pickup truck. Traffic came to a sudden standstill while the entrance gates were forced open. Emergency sirens and loudspeakers clashed over the airwaves.

"Where's Dad and the professor?"

Their vehicle had also vanished in the confusion. Kevin steered the professor's car into the outgoing lane. Pieces of the salvaged electronic gear swayed loosely in the back.

"Nothing sudden," cautioned Thor.

"Safe all the way home," Kevin promised. A flash of lightning beamed across the sky. It was followed by a roll of thunder, not unlike the blast which had first sent the workers running. Late afternoon darkness set in under heavy rainclouds. Sheets of rain washed down on the earth.

"What's happening? First, those explosions at the plant. An alert sends us running, and now this," Kevin muttered. "It's enough to ruin my day!"

With the windshield wipers at full speed, the car crawled along in the slow lane of traffic. More lightning bolts flashed overhead. The storm center was drawing closer, signaled by the increasing volume of thunder. Thor reached for the mobile cellular radio. A flick of the transceiver button brought no response from his father's frequency code. He checked other wavelengths, but they weren't functioning either.

"Must be the storm," he concluded. "A sudden discharge of atmospheric electricity can do wacky things to communications."

"Your father and the professor probably don't even realize we got stuck behind. Maybe we'll pass them before we get into Stanton."

The thought appealed to them. If they got home before the professor, they'd have a chance to unload his car before he arrived. That meant extra time for him to explain the Fission Tracer salvaged from Master Control.

"Is that an accident up ahead?" muttered Kevin.

A long bend in the expressway went through part of a valley. Flashing lights shone through the steady downpour. Traffic again came to a standstill, but they still couldn't see what was responsible for the slowdown.

Thor glanced in the video RearVu screen. Mounted in the dash panel, it indicated traffic approaching from behind. One vehicle was continuing to move despite all the other cars that were stopped.

"Anxious driver. . .must be taking the shoulder."

It was a risky way to cut through the jam. As the vehicle rumbled by them on the narrow shoulder, they could positively identify the pickup truck.

"Them again!" exclaimed the boys.

The two technicians from the station proceeded on, the low-slung rear portion of their truck indicating that they were still carrying a heavy load.

Without any prodding from Thor, Kevin pulled the professor's car out of the stalled lane. He followed the pickup truck at a safe distance. The rain increased to a torrent. The flashing lights at the bend came into focus.

A Highway Patrol roadblock!

"I can't wait until they pull our friends over," Kevin smiled.

But when the pickup drew near the roadblock, the youths witnessed an odd event. One policeman approached the vehicle, a short exchange followed, the officer laughed, and then waved the pickup through.

"Can you believe that?" whistled the boy. "We should be so lucky."

They were not. A brief look inside their car gave the officer enough reason to order a detailed interrogation. Other policemen came over to inspect the vehicle.

"Where did you get that electronics material?" demanded a lieutenant.

No explanation satisfied the officers.

The lieutenant listed the facts impatiently. "You're driving a vehicle registered to a Professor Alan Coleman. You're both still in high school. And you're loaded up with microtechnology for which you have no permit."

After every honest answer had been exhausted, Thor decided to notify another authority. The lieutenant in charge of the roadblock took the request. Using the wavelength restricted to law enforcement agencies, he reached the Stanton Police headquarters.

"Sergeant Dalby, please," he requested.

Thor and Kevin exchanged a knowing smile. Not only was the Stanton police officer a family friend, but they had assisted him in earlier cases.

"Sorry for the holdup," the lieutenant said, a minute later. "We have orders to check all vehicles coming through."

The youths felt relieved. But their curiosity had been stirred.

"What exactly are you after?" wondered Kevin.

"I wish I knew," confessed the man. "Some kind of suspicious cargo is being shipped."

"That's the reason for the roadblock?" asked Thor.

"Yeah, we're trying to track it down, but we haven't had much luck so far. Maybe it was a false alarm," the officer continued, "but we can't afford to take chances."

The youths returned to the professor's vehicle. Kevin started the ignition, checked the lanes in front and in back through the RearVu screen, then pulled away.

The rain continued to stream down. The steady sweep of the windshield wipers provided the background to the boys' discussion of the events of the day: the steel cylinder casing Kevin had found in the elevator, the guard pointing his weapon, the worker dangling from the tower, Thor pushing Kevin from the path of the speeding truck, the two odd technicians. As the youths contemplated the meaning of it all, Thor's attention was drawn to the upcoming highway entrance ramp.

"There they are!" he pointed.

Sure enough, it was the two technicians in the pickup. They were reentering the highway. By the level position of the vehicle, it was apparent that their steel cylinder had been unloaded.

"I wonder where they're coming from," said Kevin.

He quickly signaled to exit and swung the professor's car into the side lane, its load of electronic gear creaking in the back. The boys found that this ramp brought them to a desolate country road.

Thor asked Kevin to stop while he watched to see where the pickup truck was going. Through the misty rain, he saw it pull onto the highway and drive back in the direction of the Emerald Nuclear Generating Station.

From where they had stopped, the boys could see that forests and scrubland ranged over the places not cleared for farming. There seemed to be few houses located nearby. As the boys drove slowly down the road, they saw a truck pulling out of a long, tree-lined lane. Their RearVu screen froze the departing image as it went past them.

The truck's mudflaps carried the triple white pyramid design.

"Does that register?"

"It's the same truck that nearly killed me," breathed Kevin. "That's enough of a reason to check this place out."

Private Property — No Trespassing! warnings were posted on each side of the entrance to the private road. The boys ignored them as they sped along past the towering trees that acted as storm barriers. The wind pulled fiercely at the branches, but the rainfall was less vicious.

Bang! A thunderclap boomed down!

"Yikes!" screamed Kevin.

He lost control of the wheel. The car swung to the side. Its tires tore into the loose gravel, it swerved, and slid to a stop. The professor's car was stuck in the ditch!

"You've really done it now!" Thor grumbled.

"It wasn't my fault! That thunder threw me off!"

Despite Kevin's excuse, nothing could change the very difficult position the boys were in. They were stranded in a thunderstorm, on private property, in a ditch, with a car that was not theirs.

"Who walks?" asked Thor.

Bang! Another thunderclap sounded overhead. A gust of wind swept upwards, as if being sucked into the dark clouds.

"That's what made me lose control," shouted Kevin. As the rain pounded harder on the stalled car, he sought a fast solution. "Try the cell."

He was referring to the mobile cellular radio. It had worked earlier in the day when the professor had been called back to the plant by Ray Ginsler. However, it had not functioned since the electrical storm set in.

"Still no action," Thor groaned, after several attempts. "Let's both walk."

"But we'll get drenched."

From the back seat, Thor pulled two thick plastic sheets they had used to wrap the electronics gear.

"May as well put it to use."

The youngsters stepped out into the storm. They sensed the charged atmosphere that pervaded the area. Thick, low-hanging clouds moved ominously, ready to unleash more thunderclaps. Together, the boys headed down the tree-lined laneway. There was no sign of life around them. Further rumblings came from the sky, but none as terrifying as the one that had caused Kevin to lose control. Through the tempest they trudged, the plastic sheets clasped tightly about them.

They halted at a rise in the road, where a peculiar section of land stretched in front of them. A scrap metal yard was enclosed in a ring of corrugated fencing.

"A home for dead cars," sneered Kevin. "Funny, how I should run off the road that leads here."

Hundreds of rusted automobiles were stacked throughout the area. Twisted pieces of metal dumped from construction projects dotted the ground. Abandoned oil drums loomed menacingly at one end of the property. Their paint had peeled off, leaving the contents of each a mystery.

Cautiously, the boys approached the main entrance. A shaky wire gate was open, but no one seemed to be in the vicinity. The sound of rain pelting on metal filled the air.

"There must be a tow truck here," said Thor. "Or a forklift. They'd need it to move all this junk around."

"Anything. I'll try anything to pull the professor's car out."

By this point, their feet were caked in muck. The steady downpour had mixed the dirt and oily mud into a soggy mess. The junkyard resembled a pigsty. Walking became an effort.

"Well, take a look at that!" Thor said in surprise, peering from underneath his plastic sheet.

Above what had to be the yard's office was painted a familiar sign.

"Three white pyramids," whispered Kevin.

A knock at the door of the shack brought no response. Pushing the latch open, they saw a pile of garbage strewn across the floor. Along with the horrible smell, out came a huge rat!

"Yow!" they screeched, jumping back.

The rat scurried outside, to disappear under the shack's foundations.

The boys retreated over toward a large open shelter. They had to step over various pieces of rusting construction equipment, but it was worth the effort. The slanted roofing gave them cover and a chance to shake off their plastic sheets.

"What a miserable place," shivered Kevin.

The unrelenting cold was getting to them. Thor surveyed the area. They were surrounded by the castoff scraps of progress, the leftovers of planned obsolescence. Yet bordering these few acres of the junkyard, lay cultivated fields for agriculture.

"This is one of the last places I'd expect to find a scrap metal yard," he said. "Right in the middle of a farming area. Kind of strange." Rain hammered on the roofing. The youths were chilled to the bone and feeling very uneasy.

"At least we've figured out where that triple pyramid sign is from," Thor concluded after a long silence. "But that brings up a whole other worry."

"What are you talking about?"

"The last place we saw three white pyramids was on those trucks' mudflaps, and they were hauling things from the dismantled nuclear plant...."

The connection dawned on Kevin. He completed Thor's thoughts "...which means a lot of dangerous waste material. Radioactive debris."

The boys were frightened. That nuclear waste may have been dumped on the site added to their crisis. They tried wiping the thought from their minds, so that they could decide what to do.

Kevin Powell and Thor Benson squinted through the driving rain at the lifeless tools of their society. They felt as if they were the last persons on earth, watching over the remnants of a destroyed civilization.

# CHAPTER 4
# Winch Way Out

"Let's head out of here," Thor finally said.

Kevin agreed readily. They held the plastic sheeting securely over their heads and stepped back into the storm. Thickened muck squished up around their feet. The steady rain, discarded oil, and whatever other liquids had been dumped in the yard, had caused a mess that would trap even the most rugged trucks.

"What's that look like to you?" Thor indicated.

"Hmm. Maybe a hand winch?"

Thor jumped onto a nearby scrap heap and yanked the metallic device loose. Strands of wiring fell away. The boy raised it like a trophy won after a sports victory.

"Our ticket home!" he shouted.

Kevin did not yet comprehend his friend's plan. That often happened, but he usually went along with Thor and found that things worked out in the end. Both boys believed that trusting instincts was a key to their success in solving problems or mysteries.

"Help me get this together."

Kevin unraveled a batch of steel cable and, when Thor was satisfied with the length, they dragged it together from the scrap metal yard.

By the time they had made the trek back to their car, they were thoroughly soaked. The plastic sheet had blown off them as they lugged their rescue gear.

"Just get it in the right order," Thor directed. "We'll be out of here soon."

Kevin followed his instructions. He connected the steel cable between the trees on the far side of the laneway. In the center spot, Thor attached the hand winch. Next, they ran more steel cable from this connection point and wrapped it around the front drive shaft of the car.

"Now take it slow and easy. We don't want to uproot a tree," Thor yelled to Kevin behind the wheel.

While Thor stood beside the hand winch, Kevin started up the car and gently touched the accelerator.

The Y-shaped cable arrangement began to function. Thor slowly cranked the levers on the winch. It was the pivot position for the maneuver. The car's drive shaft drew in the steel cable. As pressure increased on the trees tied across the laneway, they began to creak. Slowly, the car began to move.

"What a system!" Kevin rejoiced.

"What a driver!" replied Thor.

Steadily, the vehicle pulled itself out of the ditch. Thor loosened the cable and winch, then placed them back by the tree.

In the car, the boys removed their mud-caked shoes.

"Let them dry on the floor," Kevin suggested.

Driving now in socks, Kevin put the car into reverse and backed carefully down the tree-lined laneway.

"Want to try again?" motioned Kevin.

Thor reached for the mobile cellular radio. He pressed the button and heard a new sound. The normal squawking of the tuned wavelengths came through the speaker.

"Just as the storm is letting up," Kevin commented, while switching off the windshield wipers. "Ever notice how the rain never stops when you're outside getting soaked?"

Thor laughed at his friend's theory. He wondered if it was a new subsection of Murphy's Law.

"Thor, is that you?" Mrs. Benson's voice crackled through the speaker.

"Yes, Mom. I'm in Professor Coleman's car with Kevin. We had, uh, a slight delay. Had to stop for the storm to blow over."

"You've had us worried," she said, in a tone that carried her concern over the many miles between them. "Your father and the professor are here already and are unloading all that junk of yours."

Kevin gave him a nudge. Mrs. Benson's disdain for collecting more equipment was well known. She maintained that Thor and her husband already had enough "useless junk" stored in the workshop.

"Why you need more of that stuff, I can't imagine," she continued. "Anyway, they're both out in the workshop. I'll tell them you'll be back soon."

"All right, Mom, thanks. Will dinner be ready then?"

There was silence at the other end. Suddenly, a prolonged, raspy voice began filtering through the car speaker.

"Whooooo! Food, food, don't be rude!"

Kevin glanced over at his friend. Thor shook the microphone as if to try and knock the strange voice out. The cellular radio got a tap on the side.

"Must be interference," Kevin said.

The raspy voice broke through again. "Whoooo! Interference? What's the difference?"

"Pamela!" the youths yelled together.

"Get off that line, Pammy!" her brother demanded.

"Why should I?" she teased.

"Because if you don't, I'll make sure your boyfriend here finds out what you asked me not to tell."

"But you promised!" the girl's voice protested.

"Okay, that's it. Hey, Thor, did you know that in my sister's room she has . . . "

"Kevin! I'll kill you!" shrieked Pamela.

"Stop that now!" Mrs. Benson's voice broke in. "You'll blow out these speakers! All right, Pam. Now you boys drive home safely. Goodbye!"

Thor shifted in his seat as he replaced the microphone. He continued looking ahead while contemplating the day's events. Meanwhile, Kevin decided to bring back the most recent subject.

"What are you going to do about my sister?"

Thor tried to let the question slide past. It was an inevitable topic that kept coming up. Because he had a shy nature, and Pamela Powell was a longtime neighbor, she was the only girl he felt really comfortable with. But not in the "deeply romantic sense," as others called it. Sure, he did feel certain things for the girl, some of which he told her.

"Do you want me to marry her?"

The suggestion almost sent Kevin swerving off the road.

"Watch it!" warned Thor. "Can't use thunder as an excuse anymore."

"You just let it off in here! What did I hear you say?"

"About me and Pam getting married?"

The jaw on Kevin's face was ready to fall to his chest. He gripped the wheel tighter.

"Yeah, Pam and me," Thor played along. "After all, we have so much in common. We're both fifteen years old. Still going to the same high school, even share some of the same classes. Right?"

Kevin gave a slight nod, probably more of a twitch, in response.

"Hey, Kev, I don't even have a driver's license. Why would I want a marriage license?"

The joke was up. Kevin smirked. "Man, what are you having me on like that for?"

"Because you and a bunch of other bananas keep pestering us about going together. Most of the time we ignore it. But it gets to me! We're having a good time the way we are, can't you see? Nothing's official. Nothing's wrong. Why don't you let us find out what we want? Then, maybe, we'll let you know."

For the first time in ages, Kevin felt uncomfortable with his best friend.

"Sorry for upsetting you."

"Sure. Let's keep our heads on."

They rode along the expressway in silence. Only the wind that whirled through a side vent broke the quiet. Thor wondered about some of the outdated microtechnology units they were carrying. Kevin concentrated on driving and on the electronic billboards mounted near the road. These restaurant advertisements were his food for thought.

Before long, the boys were back to their regular selves. After such a tense and unexpected day, they were looking forward to settling in safely at home. Mostly, they longed for a shower and warm clothing.

"Blast!" Kevin seethed. "What have I done now?"

Thor straightened up when his friend pointed to the video RearVu screen. Its WARNING light was flashing, and a Highway Patrol car was racing up behind them.

"But I wasn't speeding, Thor, was I?"

No sooner were his words spoken, than Kevin was forced to pull aside. He swerved onto the shoulder of the highway as a sleek sports car tore past them.

"It's Mills!" Thor shouted in recognition.

"Who?"

"The guy with the brushcut, Douglas Mills! The guard who pulled the gun on you!"

As the sports car flew by in the express lane, Kevin checked the RearVu screen again. The WARNING indicator was still flashing.

Suddenly, the Highway Patrol car raced past. The officer had a fierce challenge pursuing the swift sports car. The chase continued, as both vehicles vanished into the distance.

"Super turbocharged!" grinned Kevin, as he pulled back onto the pavement.

"I knew the professor didn't have one installed," Thor added with relief. "That's why I agreed to come back with you."

He was only half joking. Kevin Powell's reputation as a fast driver was known to many. Fortunately, his safety record was just as notable. He had combined those talents last year delivering pizzas for the Big Byte. A popular eatery with the young in Stanton, "The Byte" featured sizzling slabs of pizza. Kevin could pick up, drive, and deliver to customers before the pepperoni settled onto the crust. Nobody had timed his actual deliveries, it was claimed, because nobody dared ride with him. A few close calls and several mixed orders had slowed him down and lost him his job.

It had been many hours since they had left the Emerald Nuclear Generating Station, and they were glad to be nearing their home town.

They both loved the approach to Stanton from the elevated motorway. The modern steel and glass buildings shone like a collection of jewels on the green velvet of the surrounding pasture lands. The general store, post office, and dozen houses of the original village had been buried in the development that had accompanied the microelectronics boom of ten years ago. The high-tech firms that had required greater laboratory and warehouse space than the industrial parks of the 1960s and '70s could supply, had built a new city in the middle of an agricultural area. Though much farmland was lost to these new industries, there was some benefit to the farms that remained. Technicians took an interest in the farming process and developed better crop management systems, so that these farms now produced five times their former yield.

Kevin Powell drove toward the exit for Matrix Boulevard. Thor continued to gaze over the town, thinking how fortunate he was to live here. Why, anytime he wished, he could pass by a research lab where the latest space satellite was being developed and, five minutes later, be standing in the middle of a field with a herd of cows!

Sometimes he found the cows more fascinating than computers, but that was probably because he was not a full-time farm boy.

"We're getting close," Kevin said anxiously.

He steered onto the ramp that descended from the motorway.

"We'll unpack the gear later," suggested Thor as they turned onto their street.

As they drew nearer to 208 Matrix Boulevard, they noticed a sleek sports car parked in front of Thor's house. It was the very car that had raced past them, pursued by the Highway Patrol!

"Pull into your driveway," advised Thor.

Since the Powell home was across the road from the Bensons', they thought such a move would give them time to analyze the situation. The wet and tired boys left their mud-caked shoes in the car and climbed out in their socks.

They came up the sidewalk just in time to see Douglas Mills emerge from the house. Behind the brushcut man was Ray Ginsler, and they were both clutching brown cylinder casings under their arms. The same casings used for shipping radioactive fuel rods!

## CHAPTER 5

# Home Circuits Heat Up

"We double-checked the instruments you took from Master Control," Ray Ginsler informed the surprised youngsters. "Professor Coleman did not advise me of your extensive salvaging."

Douglas Mills tapped the cylinder casing. "This was lodged in one of the box panels."

The youths denied any knowledge of its presence.

"It makes us wonder what else might have, shall we say, slipped out, the front door," Ginsler added.

"The professor okayed everything," countered Thor Benson. "And we never packed any of those cylinders!"

The men from the Emerald Nuclear Generating Station said that all the equipment had been checked. Nothing else had to be removed.

"That's all there is?" asked Mills, indicating the Bensons' workshop.

Thor nodded, while Kevin Powell remained motionless.

"I'm sure you understand," Ray Ginsler muttered, as they turned to head back to their car.

Kevin forced himself not to mention their erratic driving. The sooner they were gone, the better.

"You didn't tell them about the professor's car," said Kevin, once the men had left. "It's loaded with stuff."

His friend shrugged. "If it really is vital, they'll get it back. In the meantime, let's find out what might be so important to them."

They entered the house together. Mrs. Benson was the first to see them.

"Thor! You are absolutely filthy! And Kevin, you're no example of cleanliness either! Get yourself home and changed! I'll run a bath for you, young man."

There was no arguing. Mrs. Benson kept her house as tidy as a model suite. That attitude also carried over into her personal lifestyle. As the college sweetheart of Edward Benson, Laraine had aged gracefully in the years since their marriage. Her work as a phys-ed instructor at the Flexercise Center kept her in top shape. She expected the same of her husband and son, who were so similar in their own activities.

Kevin retreated across the road to his own house. Meanwhile, Thor shook off the cold with a warm steam-bath. Later, relaxed and refreshed, he felt prepared to examine the additions to his workshop.

This laboratory, built into the rear of the garage, was a home-based scientific center of discovery. Though intended for his son, Mr. Benson often used the room when not at BenDaCon, his electronic data consultancy office in Stanton. When Thor appeared at the door, he found Edward and the professor in an animated conversation.

"You had some visitors?" he asked.

"Quite unexpected ones," replied the professor. "You'd think we had absconded with the Crown Jewels."

"Where did they find the cylinder casings?" the boy asked.

The men exchanged bemused glances. Each seemed to dare the other to speak.

"They probably slipped them out of their jackets," Professor Coleman said. "That is, we believe Mr. Ginsler and Mr. Mills needed to find 'something peculiar.'"

"You mean it was a setup?"

"That's right, son. For some reason, they believed we might have taken something of importance. But they couldn't find it. And so they wouldn't leave looking foolish, they planted the cylinders."

Once more, the workings of the adult mind confused the boy. What would motivate those men to lie? Why didn't they simply say what was missing? If people would try not to complicate matters so often, maybe the world would seem less like an unsolvable puzzle.

"Anyway, we sorted through a good bit of this material," the professor stated. "Some of it may have to be junked, but there's enough to keep you busy for a few months."

"Anything real special?"

"That you have to discover yourself. But if you get lost in a loop, I'm sure your father will help out."

"As usual," Edward smiled.

In the corner, two boxes of computer printout paper were being sorted. This activity, too boring for any human to undertake, was being handled by the next best thing — Mr. Chips.

"You've reactivated him," blurted Thor on seeing his domestic robot.

"Thank the professor."

"His encoder was out of alignment," shrugged Coleman. "Nothing serious, really. I used to have the same problem with mine. Your Mr. Chips must have had a fall recently."

Keeping track of the robot was less difficult than caring for a house pet, which was how the family thought of Mr. Chips. Manufactured by Thor and his father out of spare parts, retractable wheels, levers, and a programmed microcircuitry assembly, Mr. Chips was an invaluable aid to them. A specialist in home security and surveillance, Mr. Chips's capacity as a stand-alone transceiver had featured in an earlier MicroKidz mystery, *THE CAGEY BEE BYTE.*

"Maybe he can unload the rest of the stuff from the professor's car," suggested Thor.

Mr. Benson insisted he get Kevin's help instead. "Chips is doing fine right here."

When Thor tapped on the side window of his neighbour's house, Mrs. Powell waved him in. "Where did you two go today? A rodeo? I couldn't believe the mess Kevin tracked in!"

Thor joined in on the joke. "He wanted to go out to dinner, but I said you'd be upset if he didn't shower first."

"No truer words," Mrs. Powell recited. "And what did your mother have to say?"

"The same. Cold comments and a hot bath."

They enjoyed trading quips. A cheery woman, the mathematics teacher at Stanton High School, Kay Powell was popular with the youngsters. A divorced single parent, she raised Kevin and Pamela with a joy for life that ignored her earlier marital unhappiness. Thor had been much younger when Mr. Powell had abandoned his family, but he could remember his own parents consoling Kay Powell. She had picked up her life, resumed her teaching career, and become a fine example of perseverance.

"I came across a test-market floppy diskette," she said in her offhand way. "An EduComp system for math and chemistry classes. If you want to scan it, be my guest."

"That would be great!"

"But you'll have to get it off Pamela. She wanted to view it first." Then, lowering her voice, Mrs. Powell confided, "Pam is taking her Public Health job very seriously. I'm waiting for her to close down this kitchen and quarantine the house."

"I heard that!"

They turned as Pamela entered. The dark-haired girl of fifteen bore a strong resemblance to her brother around the eyes. For once, she was not smiling.

"Are you making fun of my work?" she asked.

"No. Your Mom was saying how serious you are. That's good. Isn't the Public Health for the public good?"

Thor changed his mind about kidding Pam when he saw that something was really troubling her.

"Did you see where I left the Geiger Scanner? I set it down and forgot where," Pam nervously told them. "It has to go back with me for the evening shift."

Mrs. Powell shrugged. "Did you check the side porch?"

"Mom! I'd never leave that outside!"

She searched through the room, blocking Kevin as he entered.

"Hey Thor, did you thank her for the quack call? 'Interference? What's the difference?'" he repeated, using her strange voice from the cellular radio.

The girl ignored him and left the kitchen. She was too worried about the missing Geiger Scanner to bother with Kevin's teasing.

The two youths went outside to unload the salvaged goods. Kevin removed both pairs of muck-filled shoes from the car floor and set them down on the side porch beside a round leather bag labelled G.S.

Since the workshop was best approached from the Bensons' garage, Kevin set the vehicle in neutral. It drifted silently down and across Matrix Boulevard, stopping in the opposite driveway.

The boys laid armfulls of equipment on the floor of the workshop. Professor Coleman surveyed their condition and sorted components into related groups.

"If you plan to start up your own nuclear station here, fellows, you're going about it in the right way," the elderly man chortled. "I haven't seen so many communications gizmos in one place at one time since that prank at M.I.T.!"

Even Mr. Benson laughed at this reference to the most famous, high-tech practical joke ever pulled. Thor and Kevin had yet to hear the complete version. Each time someone began to tell it, he broke into hysterics before the punch line. And now it happened again.

"Will somebody ever let us in on it?" wondered Thor, while the men continued to guffaw.

"Another time," promised his father.

Cataloguing and registering the new equipment became the first order of business. A fresh floppy diskette was popped into the drive near the desktop RND microcomputer. Thor logged on and typed "I.D.: EMERALD...USED PARTS" to code the entry. In this slow initial process, every salvaged piece was identified. Mr. Benson gave a brief description to cross-reference the input.

"Keep pressing the top," Thor advised Kevin.

Kevin was busy running an ultraviolet laser light pen across each piece. This served a dual purpose; the laser recorded all the information Thor entered in the RND micro directly onto the piece. It also imbedded a secret code, something which had been done to all the equipment in their workshop.

"What about this, Professor?"

In his hand, Edward held the Fission Tracer, its ruby-coated metal enclosed in the crystalline case. The exact use of the device remained a mystery to the boys.

"As I said in the control room, Edward, that requires a steady stream of fission emissions. I'm not sure that it will have any use in a domestic setting."

At that moment, Mr. Chips dropped the final sheet of printout paper into a bin. As programmed, the robot moved to its resting place. In doing so, it bumped into Professor Coleman.

"Here, give that Tracer to me," the older man said.

He took the Fission Tracer, its design alone worthy of display in an art gallery, and placed it atop Mr. Chips. Standing on guard by the workshop door, the little robot now had a special glow about it. The Fission Tracer unit adorned Mr. Chips like a piece of exotic jewelry.

"That might be the best use for it," the professor chuckled. "But if there's anything else you can adapt it to, go right ahead. And since you seem to be restoring order, maybe I should be on my way."

"Not so soon," Edward countered. "Laraine has prepared something special for you."

With genuine thanks from the boys, Professor Coleman left with Mr. Benson.

"What a whizzbang!" Kevin declared. "The intensity that just surrounds the guy! I bet old Einstein had the same effect."

"Must be a trait all physicists share. You can't sit around breaking up bits of the universe without it having some kind of personal effect," Thor guessed.

They continued registering and laser-labeling the gear for another hour. By this point, the youngsters were anxious to put some of it to use. Surrounded by so many choices, they felt perplexed. Finally, Kevin came up with a solution.

"Let's try a bit of deductive reasoning."

"Just what I expected to hear from the son of a math teacher."

"No, I mean in a police detective sense," Kevin clarified. "Why don't we put ourselves inside the minds of Ray Ginsler and Doug Mills."

Thor was not impressed.

"Listen, they came here today looking for something really important, something they didn't want anyone to have. What might it be?" persisted Kevin. "Deduce that first. Then put it to use."

Talk about a puzzle! Yet this was exactly the kind of mind teaser on which the MircoKidz thrived; a problem that required some lateral thinking with an off-the-wall solution.

On the floor, Kevin sorted through the stack of peripherals marked "INTERFACERS." He held up a bent digital device.

"Check this thing."

Using the laser feedback, Thor scanned the cross-reference computer listings. The INSTANT INDEX feature he had personally developed speeded up the search-and-find process. He typed several catch phrases onto the keyboard and, with a whistle of approval, read the results.

"DENSITY JITTER READER."

"What did your Dad say it was for?"

"It says here," Thor began, leaning forward to read the column off the display monitor, "DECIPHERS ANY BRIEF INSTABILITY OF A SIGNAL, PARTICULARLY ALONG COMPRESSED INTEGRATED CIRCUITS."

"Yeah. Sure."

"Okay, Kevin. In plain English, it sort of means that what you have in your hands was an important device fifteen years ago. Back then, it was probably a control unit in the nuke plant, letting the operators know of slight on-line changes."

"So why would Ginsler and Mills want it?"

Thor shrugged. "Why would you?"

A period of silence followed as they contemplated.

"Wanna know something, Thor? Maybe this deductive reasoning doesn't apply right now."

That Kevin should give up so easily made his friend react impulsively. Taking the nearest wad of paper, Thor beaned it over. Kevin's catch was just as swift. As he toppled sideways, he knocked into Mr. Chips.

Already, Thor was in motion. He grabbed the falling Fission Tracer.

It was a significant catch. Not only was the device saved from destruction, but the boys' attention was now refocused. Perhaps this was the reason Ginsler and Mills had rushed from the Emerald Nuclear Generating Station!

"Is it?"

"Remember, they only saw what was in this room before we arrived."

"While the Fission Tracer was still packed in the professor's car."

They were back to the initial question. Why would those men want it?

"Anybody home?"

The door creaked open. Pamela Powell peered into the workshop and was surprised by the strange scene before her. Her brother was stretched on the floor, holding a wad of paper in one hand and a metal device in the other. Thor Benson was on his knees, clutching a crystalline case that contained a ruby-coated metal.

"Are you guys playing charades?"

The boys stood up and enthusiastically recounted the results of their deductive reasoning. When they had finished, they waited for her response. Pamela was not interested.

"I can't think about that now," she told them. "Something more important has come up. Can you tell me exactly where you were today?"

Kevin glanced at Thor. "What's that got to do with the Fission Tracer? You know that we went with his Dad to the nuclear station."

"Is that where you got all the muck on your shoes?"

The boy laughed. "Hah! Is Mom mad at me for messing them, Pammy? That's what they make shoe polish for, you know."

"I'm serious, Kevin."

Pam's stern expression warned Thor that she was really worried about something. He intervened. "What is it, Pam?"

"Did you get all that dirt on your shoes at the nuclear plant?" she asked again, more deliberately.

"No, we didn't," Thor spoke up. "We got stuck in a lane near some scrapyard. Why?"

"Do you know the exact location of that place?"

"What is this? A police investigation?"

"Kevin, I'm not kidding around. Come on."

The girl turned and left. Their curiosity aroused by her questioning, Kevin and Thor followed her, shutting the digital deadbolt lock on the way out.

Not a word was exchanged as Pamela led the pair across the road. Streetlights illuminated the neighbourhood with a warm glow. With its wide lawns and plush homes, this part of Stanton felt very safe.

As they neared the side porch of the Powell home, Pam spoke in a whisper. "I don't want Mom to hear."

She pointed at the two pairs of muck-caked shoes lying on the porch where Kevin had left them. Alongside was an open, round leather bag labeled G.S. Inside it was a gadget resembling a voltage tester.

"Remember when I was looking for my Geiger Scanner?"

"Then Mom said, 'Look on the side porch,' and you said you'd never leave it there?" prodded Kevin. "So it looks like you were wrong!"

"Lucky for you both! I use it for the Health Department to check levels of radiation at city companies," she said softly. "Step up and look at the meter."

Uneasily, Thor and Kevin crept forward. They stared in alarm at the probe-like attachment leaning against their muddy shoes.

The meter on the Geiger Scanner was buried in the EXTREMELY DANGEROUS zone!

# CHAPTER 6
# Input/Output

Pamela Powell reported for the evening shift at the Public Health Department. This glass-walled structure was tucked into the "old" part of Stanton, even though the building had been erected just one year prior to the influx of the high-tech firms.

As usual, Kevin drove her to work in his sports car. In an unusual development, however, both he and Thor accompanied the girl inside.

The boys carried a heavy lead-lined bag between them. Pamela held the round pouch containing the Geiger Scanner. It had proved its worth in an unexpected moment.

Several students from Stanton High School and a nearby college were also employed by the Public Health Department. As part of the school-workplace semester program, the young people were making use of a great opportunity. They were combining their studies with real experience in the working world, helping them choose careers while still attending school. Many other Boards of Education around the country came to Stanton to learn how this system functioned.

"Doesn't seem to be much happening," said Thor as he looked down the vacant hallways.

"You should see it during the day," Pam explained. "Like a beehive. At night, they only have a skeleton staff."

"And they work best on Hallowe'en, right?"

Pam and Thor had heard that joke too many times to laugh at it again.

"This is my area," she said, directing them to a smaller department. The sign above the entrance read Industrial Monitoring.

Two attendants nodded at Pamela as she came through the glass door. When they saw the boys following, they looked surprised.

"Show and Tell tonight, Pamela?" asked the older man.

"Quiet, Harry. They're lending a hand."

These sympathetic words came from a woman working nearby. She was nearing sixty years of age and wore the blue smock of a senior lab technician. Pamela introduced her as Dr. Skyne.

"What's in the takeout baggy?" Dr. Skyne inquired with a smile.

Thor and Kevin set the lead-lined sack onto a table. Because this was Pamela's territory, they had agreed to let her handle the questions.

"I'd like to have the contents examined inside the Radiation Chamber."

"What's in there?" asked Harry. The technician was now showing interest.

"Two pairs of shoes," replied Pam.

"Hmmm. What about the socks?"

"Harry! Get back to your Spectralizer!" ordered Dr. Skyne. The woman was clearly in command of this department. She looked up at Kevin and Thor, although her question was directed at Pam. "And why do you think they have to be examined in the Chamber?"

"Well, Dr. Skyne, I accidentally left the probe of my Geiger Scanner near these shoes. When I checked later, the meter was registering Extremely Dangerous."

This explanation satisfied the woman. On a desktop BEN-2 computer, she ordered up the night's schedule and filed a reservation time.

"We have the Chamber in ninety minutes," she reported.

Pamela turned to the boys. "No need for you to hang around. Thanks."

Becoming very professional in her manner, she dismissed them politely. As the boys left the industrial monitoring section, Kevin glanced back through the glass doors and saw his sister helping Dr. Skyne lift the lead-lined bag onto a trolley.

Walking out into the fresh evening air, a familiar sensation came over Kevin.

"I just remembered something I forgot."

"That's usually what people remember, Kevin."

"I haven't eaten!" The boy appeared shocked at his discovery. "With all the excitement of getting back, unloading, and cataloguing, I neglected my appetite!"

Thor, too, admitted he was hungry. There was only one remedy for a colossal hunger.

The Big Byte offered lots of great fast food at low prices. Thick sandwiches, pizza, and frothy fruit shakes were the house specialties. Its location near Stanton High School had made "The Byte" a student hangout. Where else, Kevin often said, could you enjoy a hearty snack while looking over the opposite sex?

They took a booth near the door. A video monitor on

each table featured the daily menu. Once a choice was made, the correct code was punched in. This registered electronically in the kitchen, the chef read the printout sheet and sent the order through. The boys scanned the selection and went with their usuals.

"Should we go back to Pam after this?" Kevin wondered, while they waited for the food to arrive.

"Let's not put any pressure on her. She'll give us a call. Enjoy this break."

It was a good opportunity to relax. While they munched on Kilobyte Klub sandwiches, the tabletop video screen displayed the latest pop concert performances. The charge for this micro-age jukebox would be added to the bill.

Kevin tuned in the newest video by The Random Accessories. It added a pleasant backbeat to his jaw cracking, something that unnerved Thor. The most influential musical group of the times, Accessories spoke out on behalf of their generation.

"I like their stuff," said Thor.

Tall yogurt shakes washed down the quick meal. Kevin flipped a coin to decide who would pay. As usual, Thor lost.

Just as they were leaving, a police car stopped outside. They sat down again when they saw who the driver was.

"Of all people," boomed the voice of Sergeant Dalby.

They greeted the officer courteously. After pouring coffee at the take-out counter, he joined them at the booth.

"When that call came from the Highway Patrol road-block, I was almost tempted to say 'Arrest those kids!' Just for a bit of fun," he joked. "But then I thought, heck, why stir up more trouble?"

The youngsters knew the policeman well enough to detect the concern in his voice. They waited for Sergeant Dalby to continue.

"Hijackings. Grand theft," Sergeant Dalby explained quietly. "In the last two weeks, a dozen trucks and railway containers have disappeared."

"Why haven't we heard about it on the news?"

"Lots of reasons, Thor. Number one, the hijackers are still holding some drivers hostage. There are ransom demands. One rule is that the press is not to publicize the negotiations."

The man paused for a long sip of his coffee.

"What's being hijacked?"

"Anything that can be driven away. That expressway roadblock was part of the operation. We got a tip that some nuclear waste material was to be intercepted," he continued, speaking in a hushed voice. "Since the Emerald Plant has been decommissioned, it's a likely target for hijackers."

The youngsters remained silent. Lacking conclusive evidence of their own, they dared not make any premature accusations. Besides, neither Kevin nor Thor was certain that there had been any wrongdoing at Emerald.

A change of subject lightened the mood. At Sergeant Dalby's suggestion, Thor agreed to ask his father about joining in a fishing trip. These expeditions were legendary. Usually, the sergeant and Mr. Benson would charter a jet helicopter to fly them to a northern lake. When the pilot returned that evening to bring the men home, he always threatened to charge them for an extra passenger, so heavy was their catch.

"But you have to promise to take both of us," Kevin said.

"One of these days," Sergeant Dalby replied before leaving.

The final bill for the food and music appeared on the tabletop display screen. Thor inserted his Automatic

CashCard, verified his private account code, and pressed the TR button. In a nondescript building many miles away, the transaction entered a bank computer. Thor's debit became the Byte's credit.

"Where to now?"

The question was not really necessary. The other busy place in this plaza was the Arkade. Kevin knew it particularly well from a previous adventure when they had short-circuited a rigged laserdisc videogame conspiracy there.

Thor was regarded by many players as the one to challenge. His ability to beat the scores of most computer games had forced the manufacturers to alter the programs coming to this Arkade. The reason for this was simple. Thor was something of a computer genius and had himself invented *Starbryte,* one of the most popular home video games. Thor enjoyed the status his invention gave him, and money from its sales permitted him to pay for his own vacations, purchase state-of-the-art equipment for his workshop, and build his own college trust fund.

"Hey, man! When is *Starbryte* gonna have a booth here?" asked an older youth. The question was constantly being asked of Thor.

"It's not an arcade game," Thor explained for the millionth time. "The real fun, and test, of *Starbryte* comes when played at home. You need very familiar surroundings."

Kevin and Thor had decided not to call Pamela until certain the examination would be completed. In the meantime, to kill some time, they tried out two of the newest laserdisc games.

"No sweat to this," Kevin chuckled while holding the control levers for *Daze & Knights.*

"Yeah, kind of boring," was Thor's assessment of the recent version of *The Unquenchables.*

They peered over the shoulders of other players. It gave them a chance to consider the process from a programmer's perspective. They took note of each move, comment, and complaint by the players. Thor still had ideas for other computer games, and he wanted to make his the best of the batch.

"Those big manufacturers still don't know what to do," he commented as they left the Arkade.

"All they make is small refinements to the games we already know," Kevin agreed. "I tell you, there's a whole group of people out there who aren't playing because there's nothing new."

The feeling was shared. Despite being avid players themselves, the youths realized that only a loyal minority kept the games manufacturers in business.

Kevin considered the bright side. "That means there's hope for us yet!"

They drove back to Matrix Boulevard to resume organizing the workshop. Thor saw that his parents were busy inside the house and waved to them on his way out to the lab. He dialed open the digital deadbolt lock and, under the soft fluorescent lighting, the youths began to tinker again on the new equipment.

Among the more fascinating pieces was an early model Data Dispenser. A check in the RND microcomputer identified its "CAPABILITY FOR ROUTING DIFFERENT LEVELS OF DATA TO MULTIPLE END-USERS." Since that job was already being performed more efficiently by newer units, the Data Dispenser seemed destined for the junk pile. Thor, however, had second thoughts.

"Hey, that functions on transistors. Even though we've passed that scale, it might come in handy for some remote work. Set it aside."

The piece was stored in a cardboard box, joining a variety of peripherals whose purpose had yet to be determined. This was the kind of challenge Kevin and Thor loved; to develop something new out of old nothings, perhaps even something with more potential than it had initially. Why not? With time, patience, and a lot of clever thinking, they might restore these obsolete devices to life.

"I agree that Fission Tracer is best as a high-tech hat on Mr. Chips," Kevin remarked during a break.

The domestic robot remained motionless. Its programmed activity mode had been decelerated. Thor looked at the high-tech hat and wondered if indeed it was the reason Ray Ginsler and Douglas Mills had come to search the premises. What might the Fission Tracer be?

"Thor? Kevin?"

The voice outside the locked door was Mr. Benson's. He tapped at the same time as he called out, "Message inside."

Quickly, the boys shut down the workshop and followed Mr. Benson into the house.

"On the VistaPhone," he indicated before leaving to rejoin his wife.

The family's home communications base was set up in the hallway CompuCorner. By pressing the touch-sensitive screen on the VistaPhone, address codes were dialed, and the other person appeared on the monitor. When Thor returned the waiting call, Pamela became visible.

"We have the results from the Radiation Chamber," she said in a flat tone.

"Well, let's hear it."

"Sorry. Nothing can be released over this line."

"When are you coming back tonight?" Kevin asked.

Pamela seemed to evade the question. "Why don't you both get here as soon as possible?"

Out of range of the fibre-optic relay lens, Thor indicated for Kevin to delay his response. He wanted to observe Pamela's unusual mannerisms.

"So, anyways, what does Dr. Skyne have to say about you being in the shoe cleaning business?" improvised Kevin.

Pam glanced to the side, as if she was taking instructions from somebody out of lens range.

"Is Dr. Skyne still there?" Kevin persisted. "Can I talk to her?"

There was a shuffling in front of the screen. The boys watched as their VistaPhone picture went blank. Then, just as quickly, the image returned. This time, however, Dr. Skyne was sitting beside Pamela and she began to speak in an oddly cheerful voice.

"Hello, boys. We had a little transmission problem. Why don't you both come down here and we'll talk over the test results? Fine? We have to go now."

With that, the VistaPhone shut off.

"Shall we leave word?" asked Kevin in a worried voice.

Thor nodded and walked through the house to the front lounge. Mrs. Benson was holding her husband's hand as they shared a private joke. The boy felt like an intruder, but he also knew his responsibility.

"Excuse me, Mom and Dad. I'm going out with Kevin to pick up Pam at the Public Health Department. Just wanted to let you know."

At first he thought they hadn't heard him. While he stood in the doorway, his parents continued to look at each other. His father spoke up after a moment.

"That's fine, son. Take your time."

Thor returned to the CompuCorner where Kevin was fussing with the controls.

"I can't dial through to them," he said with growing concern. "We better hurry."

They ran out of the house, across the street, and into the car. Kevin had the good sense not to squeal his tires until he approached the Cartesian Freeway.

The night lights flickered below them. Most of the scenery blurred by them as the engine's super turbocharger took over. This power booster made the ride much shorter.

They pulled up in front of the Public Health building. All the interior lights were on, and nothing seemed to be out of place. As they parked the car in front of a delivery truck, Thor grabbed Kevin's arm.

"Hold back!" he whispered.

Raising his other arm, Thor pointed to a pickup truck parked by the front doors. On its rear mudflaps were the white triple pyramids!

The boys approached the entrance, taking care to keep well back in the shadows. Their thoughts were identical. Was this the same vehicle they had seen leaving the Emerald Nuclear Generating Station?

"I can't say for sure," admitted Kevin.

They didn't need to wait long for an answer. Two men emerged from the building and, in the bright light of the reception area, Thor and Kevin could see them clearly.

It was the two odd technicians from Emerald, the tall man and his bald friend. Between them, they carried Pamela's lead-lined bag!

# CHAPTER 7

# Fission Chips

The nervous technicians tossed their seized cargo into the rear of the pickup. While the bald man directed, his tall partner reversed out. Once clear, he jumped in, and they were gone.

Certain the men were not returning, Thor Benson and Kevin Powell headed straight into the Public Health Department Center. The corridors seemed eerily devoid of life.

"Which way?" Thor yelled in confusion.

"Keep it down!" Kevin warned, as he pulled him around a corner.

They found the correct route leading to the industrial monitoring glass doors. Sitting around the desk inside were Pamela, Dr. Skyne, and Harry.

"You're a bit too late," sighed Pamela.

"We tried. You mean those two..."

Kevin did not finish his statement. The visit by Emerald's technicians was self explanatory. Nevertheless, Thor demanded it.

"I had no idea they would react so quickly," Dr. Skyne explained. "They must have been in the vicinity."

"Who called them?" Kevin wondered.

"It's an automatic procedure," Harry explained, becoming quite animated. "Whenever radioactive materials register at a certain level inside the Chamber, an alarm circuit breaks into the Nuclear Regulatory Offices. They're notified automatically, in case the situation demands a fast response."

"This was a record time," Dr. Skyne muttered.

Pamela had said nothing to her co-workers or the Emerald technicians about the origin of the shoes. However, with Kevin and Thor present, the ownership was obvious.

"And where did this radioactive soil get on your shoes?" inquired the doctor.

"How do you know it really is radioactive?" challenged Kevin. "Where's the proof?"

"Our analysis from the Radiation Chamber?" Harry spoke up. "Those men took it. They seized the floppy right from our disk drive."

"That had the total computer analysis on it," Pam reported glumly.

"If I were to run off another copy, would you tell me where this soil is?" bartered Dr. Skyne. "It is a potential danger."

Pam turned to the woman. "You really have another copy?"

"What do you think would happen around here if we didn't keep a permanent records storage? Of course there's a master copy," she revealed. "Stored at half-track, inside a central magnetic drum. It's our insurance factor."

"If you do give it to us, Doctor, I guarantee that we'll take you right to the place. Okay?"

Despite Thor's earnest pleading, the woman explained the matter in a slow, deliberate manner.

"No. I don't have to go there. But for Public Health reasons, I must know!" she stressed. "Now, before I do have a copy disk of the analysis sent here, I'll tell you the results."

The sounds of other machines in the area appeared to increase in volume. Seconds dragged into unbearable lengths as they waited for the doctor to speak. She emphasized that her words must be kept in strict confidence.

"Inside the muck and dirt clinging to those shoes, we found traces of radioactive particles. Specifically, strontium 90 and cesium 137. These are fission products derived from the nuclear power generating process."

Thor and Kevin felt as if they'd been punched in the stomach. Strontium 90 and cesium 137 were two of the deadliest chemicals on earth!

"These fission particles, tiny chips actually, seem to be filings or shreddings of some kind," the doctor continued. "They might have been driven below the surface of the soil by rain and snow. At times they percolate upwards. When the soil is stirred up, these buried poisons reemerge."

A state of shocked silence lingered.

"What should they do?" breathed Pam.

"I'll call those fellows from Emerald back," advised Harry. "This is something they asked to hear about right away."

"No, please don't," Kevin protested.

Thor added his concern. "Give us two days, Dr. Skyne. We might be able to find out what's really going on."

Even Pamela put in a plea for time. The trust that the doctor had placed in the girl's work made this decision somewhat easier.

"How can I refuse the MicroKidz?"

Five minutes later, a new floppy disk copy, to replace the one seized by the Emerald technicians, was delivered up from Central Data Processing.

As the three youngsters prepared to leave, the woman called them over to a cabinet. She implored their secrecy again.

"I think that you're probably going to get close to places where you really shouldn't be. And I don't want to hear about it in advance," she added, pulling open a drawer marked Medications. She handed them a bottle containing yellow capsules. "Take these along. Pamela knows about them. She'll explain. And good luck, but be careful!"

The trio left together. Harry was sad to have all the evening's entertainment disappear at once. His superior demanded his silence on the visit. Dr. Skyne wanted no additional danger.

Holding the fresh disk in its anti-magnetic cover, Pamela followed Thor and her brother to the sports car. The conversation during the drive home was intense. First and foremost, the threat of radioactive poisoning loomed in their minds.

"It's an invisible killer," muttered Kevin.

"But not an unknown element," Pam reminded him.

"It's argued that nuclear power is a necessary evil," Thor mused. "But its wastes and byproducts are an everlasting danger. I don't know what to think about the issue."

"Maybe there's no point anyhow. The choice has already been made for you," stated Kevin. "And everyone!"

The youngsters proceeded directly to the workshop lab behind the garage. At times like this, it functioned as the perfect meeting place. Before the new disk was loaded, Pamela opened the plastic container Dr. Skyne had given them. From it, she took out two yellow capsules and handed one to each boy.

"This is potassium iodide B-3. It will counteract any illness from the fission chips."

"What are the aftereffects?" Thor asked her.

"Your appetite may increase."

"Do you think Kevin really needs that?"

"Shut your valve, Thor. And take this pill like the doctor says."

They washed the medicine down with swigs from a bottle of orange juice. Since they had been exposed to the radiation for such a short time, and because it had not directly touched their skin, Dr. Skyne had said their prospects were excellent. Her fear, however, was that they would continue their activity. And that was exactly what the inquisitive youths proposed to do. At least with the potassium iodide B-3 capsules, they had taken some preventative measures.

"Out of the way," Thor grunted.

He had picked up a K-Booster from under the communications rack. Once it was connected to his disk drive, Pamela opened the anti-magnetic carrying case.

"Our platinum record," joked Kevin, as the disk was inserted.

Thor typed his LOAD command onto the RND micro keyboard. Whirling at thousands of revolutions per second, the information stored on the disk now loaded itself into the RND's random access memory. A red light blinked merrily as the data was transferred.

"Now the K-Booster," said Thor to himself.

Using this homemade device, all the source data could be magnified exponentially. Great varieties of colors and more precise Computer-Aided Design line drawings became visible. This was an occasion that required extreme accuracy.

"Can you switch on the remote monitor?" Pam asked.

She positioned herself in front of the huge display screen on the far wall. What it normally lacked in clarity and definition would be made up for by the K-Booster.

Images rolled across both the small monitor atop the RND micro and the wall remote. Each displayed chemical formulas, spectral analysis codes, and true-life graphics of the Radiation Chamber experiments.

"Oooohh, every time I see that muck it makes me sick," Pamela squirmed.

"Then take one of your yellow capsules."

Her brother's comment was not appreciated. She blinked, watching the mud get sliced paper-thin under the power of a laser beam. At one level, little glowing dots appeared.

"That's them!" reported Pam.

Thor stopped the microcomputer display. He activated the K-Booster to enlarge and enhance the image. What they now saw was a sight so rare that three years ago it would have been called impossible. Rare isotopes of cesium 137 and strontium 90 were magnified thousands of times their natural size!

"Fission chips!" whispered Thor.

They shone more brilliantly than diamonds. Successive angles glistened at dangerous levels. Thor worried that these playback images would burn spots onto his monitor screens. Each perspective of the glowing radioactive embers dazzled the eye. It seemed as if the universe was simultaneously being created and destroyed.

"I can't take too much of this," Kevin admitted, shielding his eyes.

"It has a half-life of only thirty years," Thor remembered his father saying. "Imagine the power still available in that!"

"I prefer not to," Pam said. "What would happen if it ended up in the control of the wrong people?"

Terrible things! Nuclear waste material could produce uranium and plutonium, essential ingredients for atomic weapons. An illegal stockpile of nuclear waste was worth a fortune. Fanatical scientists, foreign dictators, terrorists, would all be eager purchasers of the chemicals.

"If fission waste products are being smuggled out of the Emerald Nuclear Generating Station, it's our duty to alert the authorities," stated Kevin Powell.

"What if they don't pay attention?"

Pamela spoke from experience. For the MicroKidz though, there was no turning back. Whatever they had accidentally uncovered in that scrap metal yard could have a global impact.

"We can't do it ourselves, though." Again, Pamela reminded them of the obvious. Kevin and Thor agreed.

"Why don't you start by telling us how this Geiger Scanner works?" asked Thor, lifting the round leather pouch.

In exact terms she outlined the features. The Scanner was a supermodified relative of the Geiger Counter. Like that early invention which had detected levels of radioactivity, the Geiger Scanner also had the capacity to measure atmospheric charges over a wide area. The principle was the same, but countless refinements surpassed all previous models.

"And with these tiny earplugs, I can hide the Scanner in my shoulder bag and take readings anywhere, without people knowing."

This capability might come in handy sometime, the youths realized.

As midnight passed, the three youngsters were still hard at work. The investigation had to be managed perfectly; they couldn't risk any loose ends. Whenever another device had to be customized, the laser lathe was put into service.

They knew it was a race against time. Their enemy was a force whose identity was unknown, but that must not stop them.

Unfortunately, Mrs. Powell did.

"Pamela! Kevin! Are you in there? It's long past midnight!"

Mrs. Powell scolded them mildly as they departed. She was more upset that they had neglected to inform her of their whereabouts than she was by the lateness of the hour.

Thor was left alone in his workshop. He replayed the video analysis portion of the disk. Explosions of sub-atomic energy filled his wall-size display monitor. Before his eyes, fission chips broke apart and, for a moment, the world seemed to stop.

# CHAPTER 8
# Increasing Danger Levels

The sports car was parked in a hidden country lane. Only an abandoned farmhouse stood nearby. From this vantage point, the MicroKidz were able to watch traffic leaving the expressway.

"How far is the nuke plant from here?" Pamela asked after awhile.

Kevin replied, "About twenty minutes."

"A bit longer if anybody else is driving," Thor clarified.

"When are we leaving?"

"Patience, Pam. We've only been here an hour."

"But my legs are getting stiff. It's no fun being crammed into the back of a two-seater when you're the third person."

"You wanted to come."

"Me? I was practically drafted! Besides, there was no way I was going to let you take the Geiger Scanner. I'm responsible for it."

The bickering continued for a short while. Thor was amused by these exchanges. While he played the role of silent observer, the brother and sister argued with each other. Was this how kids in a family normally behaved? As an only child, he'd often wondered: was he missing out by not having any brothers or sisters? Probably, but then he might be a different person today. And maybe the Powells would not be his very best friends.

Thunder rolled across the sky.

"Put your window up," he advised.

"It's not going to rain," Pam said. "There aren't any clouds."

"You weren't here yesterday. The sky drops like a waterfall around here."

They heard another rumble, but there was no lightning, nor did any rain fall.

"Weird," Thor muttered to himself.

They contemplated the rural scenery around them. Nearby fields had thrived from yesterday's nourishing rain. The expressway was the only sign of man's intrusion on the landscape.

"Check these out," said Kevin, pointing out his side window.

From the expressway exit ramp, three large trucks had turned onto the country road and were about to pass the concealed sports car. Each truck had a canvas cover over its load, probably to ensure that the shipment was not spilled or blown away. However, it was the back ends of the trucks that alerted the youths.

"Triple pyramids," breathed Kevin.

Three white pyramids on the mudflaps identified their common origin. It looked as if the boys were correct in their theory, but they had to sit tight a bit longer to get proof.

Pamela became anxious. "Come on. What's the secret about these pyramids?"

"Ever hear of Pyramid Power?" mumbled her brother.

"You mean putting fruit under them to stay fresh or getting razors sharpened?"

"Right, Pammy. Well, this is different." Kevin noticed she was not interested in his jokes right now. He shifted to the truth. "All right. The first time we noticed them was on a truck at the Emerald. I nearly got run over. Last night we saw them again. On the back of the pickup those two tekkies drove. The ones who visited you and the doctor?"

Now she understood the connection. The boys, in turn, questioned her on the remote warning system which alerted the Nuclear Regulatory Office. Where was it located in relation to the Public Health Center?

"A private building in Stanton. That's all Dr. Skyne said."

"Then how did those two from Emerald get sent to you?"

"Nobody knows," she told Kevin.

"The Regulatory Office is responsible for overseeing all nuclear activities," Thor reasoned. "Which means the agency illegally turned over that information to someone at the Emerald plant."

"Or the data was intercepted," added Pam.

Another hour passed. Finally, they saw the three trucks come back down the road. The canvas coverings were off and their loads had been dumped.

"Wait," Thor suggested.

They watched the vehicles lumber back onto the expressway ramp. Their direction signaled a return to the Emerald Nuclear Generating Station.

"Here we go!" cheered Kevin.

Kevin accelerated onto the country road. Within minutes, the youngsters had turned down the tree-lined laneway with the scrap metal yard at the far end.

"It's still there," noted Kevin, pointing to the steel cable and winch they had used to pull the professor's car from the ditch.

"I hope we won't need it this time," said Thor.

Suddenly, Pamela called out, "Hold on! Stop!"

The Geiger Scanner was operating. Kevin slammed on the brakes as Thor turned to check the Scanner with Pam.

"Don't go any further, Kevin," she warned. "There's an extremely high atmospheric count."

The Scanner's meter was fluctuating wildly. Pamela aimed the attached probe outside the car window. Every time it was directed toward the end of the road, the meter soared. The scrap metal yard was a hotbed of radioactivity!

Kevin lifted a high intensity OptoScope from his kit bag. He adjusted the rangefinder and zoomed in on the distant lot. Using this video telescope, he could record viewed images at the touch of a button.

"Something's going on up there," he reported. "Things are being moved around. They must have a crew cutting metal, moving soil, maybe cleaning up. Awfully busy."

He handed the OptoScope to Thor for his assessment. Pam continued to monitor the radiation levels with the Geiger Scanner probe.

"It's madness. Maybe even murder. Nobody can work under levels like that without dying," she maintained. "This is taking measurements a hundred feet above that yard, then comparing them to ground level figures. And it's going off the scale!"

That was enough to frighten them away. Kevin put the car into reverse. The steel cable and winch wrapped around the trees reminded him to drive safely. They encountered no traffic on the laneway or the country road.

The MicroKidz breathed easier once they had swung onto the expressway. Pamela voiced concern about their direction.

"We're going to Emerald," Kevin stated.

Thor did not disagree. Pam remained wary.

"What are you going to do there? Tell someone that waste material is being dumped illegally?"

Kevin continued driving as Thor explained their intention.

"There's only one person at the plant we can trust. Professor Coleman. And we owe it to him to pass on this information."

Pamela could see there was no point in arguing; the boys were determined to warn the professor. She packed the Geiger Scanner unit into her shoulder bag, leaned back, and tried to relax. She wondered what was going through Thor's mind. As Pam studied him sitting quietly in front, she tried to imagine him in a few years time. Would he stay in Stanton? Or would he accept one of many offers to work in a larger city? They had shared some special moments together.

"By the way, Thor. Do you have anything planned for Saturday night?"

He turned halfway round in his seat. "Why?"

"A girl in my Stats class is having a party."

Thor understood. "Oh? Sure. Maybe. It all depends."

He always does that, Pam thought to herself.

"Why haven't I heard about that party?" her brother asked.

"I just remembered it," she answered shortly.

Kevin glanced over at Thor and smiled. "See? She doesn't want me around. Isn't that right, Pammy?"

Pamela didn't like Kevin's teasing and Thor didn't want to listen to another dispute. He decided to try and stop their bickering before it developed into an argument.

"Let's not get carried away, all right? Stick to the driving, Kevin. And Pam, if we get things settled before then, Saturday night is on. Deal?"

The twin cooling towers of the Emerald Nuclear Generating Station came into view. Work crews were still dismantling parts of the reactor. Trucks bearing huge pipes shifted toward the exit. At the checkpoint, a guard ordered the sports car to stop.

"Use mine," Thor said, handing over his ID pass to Kevin.

"Who are you seeing?" the guard inquired.

"Professor Coleman," replied Kevin.

The guard took the pass, stepped back to his post, and scanned it through the Q-D-Tector. The green crystal failed to flash.

"What time was your appointment?" demanded the guard.

"We don't have one."

Again the man returned to his post. He requested a detailed check over his intercom. The guard came back and handed Kevin the ID pass.

"Go straight ahead. Parking on the left."

Minutes later, the three youngsters were sitting in a reception lounge waiting for the professor.

"I hope we're not disturbing him," Pam said to the others. "We should have called ahead. Just to be polite."

"Oh, Pammy. You're so proper."

Kevin's words were needless and hurtful. Thor knew he was feeling frustrated and decided not to say anything.

Pam tried to lighten the mood. "Do you think the professor will be surprised?"

Instead, it was their turn to be surprised. Kevin noticed the two odd technicians strolling outside toward their pickup truck. Then, before the trio could hatch a plan to investigate, another surprise came their way.

"And so we meet again," pronounced Douglas Mills.

He paced the floor of the reception lounge looking over the youngsters, marching in step to a clanging sound from the towers. His brushcut bristling under the spot lighting, Mills waited for a response.

Thor took the initiative. "Professor Coleman is on his way?"

"Shortly. When he's through. In the meantime, can I be of any help?"

"We're here on a courtesy call."

"Yes, why not?" Mills sneered. "Who knows, there may still be other equipment lying around for you to pick up."

The youngsters sat motionless. His snide remark had made them edgy.

Suddenly, a thunderous roar enveloped the area.

"Rain again, don't you think?"

Douglas Mills got no reaction to his comment. His presence was not appreciated, nor was his very small talk.

"I'll see if the professor's ready."

As the man departed, there was another thundering roar overhead. Thor went to the window and checked the sky.

"Not a rain cloud up there."

The door slid open and Professor Coleman entered. His appearance shocked the youths. He looked haggard, as if he had not slept last night. He managed a weak smile as he slumped into a chair.

"You caught me on a bad day. I've been working for hours on an incredible mix-up. I'm really in no condition to take you around."

"We only stopped by to thank you, professor. All that gear is just fabulous."

"Your father said it would be. By the way, where is he?"

Thor realized he had an opening. Since he suspected that secret listening devices might be operating in the lounge, he had been wondering how they were going to tell the professor about their discoveries. Now the professor had given him a golden opportunity.

"He's not too well, professor. In fact, we really came here to ask if you'd see him. I know a visit from you would be good for him."

Pam and Kevin sensed Thor's plan.

"But I saw him just yesterday and he looked well," the Professor said. "I'm sorry to hear he's sick. I'll call him on the VistaPhone."

"He'd really prefer to see you in person."

"Hmm. I'll try my best. But later," the man continued. "You see, today is also a dark day for us."

"Why is that, sir?"

"Three of our trucks have been hijacked."

Three trucks? Were they the same ones they had seen at the scrap metal yard? The MicroKidz were stunned.

"Almost an epidemic, this thievery. But let me check the schedule with Mr. Ginsler and see what time I might be free."

Professor Coleman walked slowly from the room. A visit from the youngsters should have enlivened him. However, all the news today seemed to have aged him.

Another roar of thunder rolled past. This time the storm center seemed poised nearby. Oddly though, there were still no threatening clouds in the sky.

Pamela looked out at the twin reactor towers. She told the boys she wanted to see them close up. This was her first time on the site; perhaps her only chance to see the towers before they were dismantled. Kevin said he would escort her.

"No, I will," offered Thor.

Before they had a chance to leave, Douglas Mills returned, holding a large envelope.

"Professor Coleman will be off in two hours. He passed on this questionnaire for you fellows to complete. It has to do with career choices."

"What about me?" wondered Pam.

"He only gave me two," Mills said shortly. "If you want I can have another copy sent. . . ."

"No, that's fine," she interjected. "While they're busy, I'll take a walk outside."

Pamela left the boys in the lounge and wandered out onto the grounds of the nuclear station. She clutched her shoulder bag tightly to her side and made sure the tiny earphone she wore was connected to the Geiger Scanner.

To Pamela Powell, the decommissioned plant was a fascinating place. The workers behaved in a carefree manner, waving at the girl as she passed by. It seemed that the dismantlement of Emerald posed no danger or threat to its crews.

She spotted the strange pair of technicians on the loading docks. They were carting a set of brown cylinder casings to their pickup truck. Lying on the ground beside the truck was her lead-lined bag!

In a daring moment, she decided to follow her instincts. She made her way quickly to the parking lot, scribbled a brief note to her brother and Thor, and left it pinned inside the sports car.

As she returned to the docks, thunder echoed again across the cloudless sky. The rumbling seemed to arouse the workers to move more briskly. Pamela recalled a previous experience with bees; changes in weather had provoked a similar excited response. But these were people she was observing, not insects.

"Stand aside!" a trucker's voice boomed.

He waved the girl onto a walkway. From here, she watched a line of trucks leaving the tunnel that stretched underground to an area between the reactor towers. This was the final loading stage for the radioactive waste.

As each truck in the procession passed by, the meter on her Geiger Scanner jumped wildly. It was certainly no coincidence that all these vehicles' mudflaps bore the design of three white pyramids.

"And still more to come," she thought to herself.

Pamela approached the edge of the loading dock, resolved to find out what those two technicians were doing with the lead-lined bag. Why did they take it from the Health Center and bring it here? And what was in the remaining cylinder casings?

Her earphones relayed silence now, the Geiger Scanner detected no further danger levels. This gave her the needed encouragement to investigate. She looked carefully to make sure she was alone, then quickly stepped up onto the dock and entered the rear of the nearest truck trailer.

Sealed drums of nontoxic fluids were stacked at one end. The Geiger Scanner hummed at a very low intensity. Even empty cylinder casings gave negative readings.

"This is clean," she said to herself. "I'll check a few other trucks."

Pam heard voices outside. The shippers were coming back! Sounds of an argument filtered through the walls. Pamela stepped into the rear of the trailer to crouch behind a metal drum.

Thud! An object was tossed onto the floor. The door was slammed shut, and the trailer became pitch dark.

Pamela's ears crackled with another sound. The Geiger Scanner was emitting a steady tone. Whatever had been thrown in must be radioactive.

As the girl tried to stay calm and think out her next

move, a diesel truck engine started up. The whole trailer shuddered as it was attached to the truck cabin. Pamela was imprisoned in a tractor-trailer shipment of nuclear waste material!

# CHAPTER 9
# Splitting the Unit

Kevin Powell glanced up from his questionnaire. Across the table, Thor Benson put his sheet aside too. He followed his friend's line of sight. Together they watched another tractor-trailer rig pull away.

"They never stop," mumbled Kevin.

"Can't, if they're behind schedule," replied Thor. He shuffled the questionnaire. "How did you do on the multiple choices?"

Kevin fingered his sheet. "Okay. Could have used some help from Pam, though."

They had no way of knowing that Pamela was trapped inside the very tractor-trailer they were watching. Unaware of the irony of his remark, Kevin said, "It's a good thing she didn't take this test. Pam would have blown the section on 'Curious Matters.'"

The project supervisor studied the confidential memo.

"That's the latest we have," Douglas Mills reiterated.

For Ray Ginsler it was not enough. "Give me an update every half hour. And see how Coleman is doing."

"What about those kids? They're upstairs taking old employment tests."

"Keeping them busy, right?" laughed Ginsler. More pressing affairs required his attention. "As soon as the results come in from the scrapyard, I want to close the deal."

Both men smiled at the prospect. The final stages of the dismantlement had begun. A critical decision awaited. The project supervisor leaned back in his chair.

"How much do you think we'll clear?"

Doug Mills grinned. "Three to four."

"Million!"

"Dollars! Each!"

Ray Ginsler picked up the white construction helmet. "Not bad for six months work."

"Part-time," added Mills.

They enjoyed the thought of easy riches together. Their decoy shipments and resales of nuclear waste products was operating perfectly.

"Check on the old man," advised Ray.

Professor Coleman sat bent over the computerized blueprint viewer. His office was a cramped space on the second floor. When Douglas Mills entered, the physicist squinted up from the desk. His whole body expressed his frustration.

"Any luck yet?"

"No, Mr. Mills. Your data input must be incorrect. I have checked and rechecked. My original calculations remain valid."

"Then where did it all go? Use another formula for decay rates."

Anger swelled up from the exhausted man. "I have applied every formula! But nothing explains the loss of half a ton of nuclear waste!"

Time to back off, Mills thought.

"Fine. I'll tell Ray of your conclusions."

"Don't bother, Mr. Mills. I have several matters to discuss with him," yawned the old man. "Why don't you send those youngsters in to me? I could use some youthful optimism now."

Mills nodded and left. As he contemplated the physicist's results, he tried to develop counter-arguments. Those statements had to sound convincing for three days. After that, he and Ginsler would be out of the country.

Forever.

"Were you challenged?"

Thor and Kevin stretched.

"Surely it wasn't that bad," suggested Doug Mills as he picked up their completed questionnaires. "This evaluation is standard throughout the industry. Even though this plant is decommissioned, we still conduct tests and refer workers."

"What about a reference to Professor Coleman?" demanded Kevin.

Mills saw their impatience. He waved the forms, and the boys followed him up to the second floor to the professor's office.

"Where's the girl?" asked Coleman.

"My sister went for a walk outside. She wanted a closer look at those towers."

"Might as well. They won't be there much longer. In fact, don't be surprised if I go before those towers!"

His statement caught the boys off guard. They could see the stress on the professor's face.

"Are you ill, sir?"

"Probably am, Thor. But I'd be the last to admit it. More likely, just plain old exhausted."

They made him settle back into his chair and poured him a glass of water. He drank it slowly. For an instant, the flicker in his eyes returned.

"Those employment tests I asked you to take. If you get a response from the Nuclear Advisory Board, ignore it. Takes a smart person to pass them, all right. But it takes a smarter person to refuse the job."

"Why shouldn't we accept an offer?" Kevin wondered. "Nuclear facilities require computer operators."

"And an iron stomach," coughed the man. "Stay around these reactors a few years and you lose your sense of discovery. Take me, for instance. Taught physics at three universities. Also, experimental nuclear assembly procedures. For a change, I accept the offer to oversee construction of Emerald. What happens? Like strontium or cesium, I don't leave!"

His choice of chemicals for examples had a special significance for the boys. Those were the fission by-products in the muck on their shoes.

"Your father had the right idea. Go in, do the job, and leave." He paused, "Oh, didn't you say he wanted to see me?"

"Yes, as soon as possible. He'd like you to visit." While speaking, Thor began to write a message on a piece of paper. He still feared the presence of a listening device. "What do you say, Professor?"

A finger to the lips alerted the old man. The professor held the paper close to his eyes: they were strained from checking the computerized blueprints all night.

"I didn't think it was that serious," he replied loudly. He had in fact read the message, but answered as though the conversation was continuing. "Are you certain?"

"Very much so."

Thor took the paper from the man and handed it to Kevin. Before ripping it up, he scanned the contents: *"Your hijacked trucks are dumping nuke waste at a scrap metal yard! Come with us!"*

"Your father and I go back a long time, Thor, even before he was married. If there's anything I can do to make him happy, I will."

The youths smiled broadly. They had his cooperation. From a desk cabinet, Professor Coleman extracted a data storage file. He handed two diskettes to Thor, who tucked them inside his shirt.

"I'll have to notify Mr. Ginsler in case he needs to contact me," the professor said, rolling his eyes in mock horror. "Wait in the parking lot."

Kevin led the way. Thor clutched the hidden diskettes and followed. When they were outside the building, they quickened their pace. They felt second in a race against time.

"What about Pam?" remembered Kevin.

"She's around somewhere. You take a look. I'll wait in the car with our little gift."

Kevin began walking toward the reactor towers. It was the most obvious point of interest for his sister. A fast survey revealed no sign of her. He did, however, note the activity on the loading dock and saw the two technicians stacking more cylinder casings.

Meanwhile, Thor had discovered Pamela's note. She claimed to be *"On the trail. Tune in homing radar to 701 mkz."* He crumpled the paper in anger.

The homing beacon radar had a range of 120 miles. A dashboard switch set the receiver in action. Steady beeps came on the screen. Thor recognized the pattern: she was in transit, heading in a northeasterly direction.

"Blast!" he yelled. "She's risking everybody."

He tucked the two diskettes under the seat. He dared not leave the car in case Professor Coleman came out. And he was afraid of what Kevin would do once he found out.

"That girl!" he muttered aloud.

He couldn't sit still. He shut down the homing radar and made certain the diskettes were secure. Then he locked the car doors and went to find Kevin.

There was no sign of the professor leaving the building. Probably still talking to Ray Ginsler, Thor thought. Surely the supervisor would accept the popular "going to visit a sick friend" excuse.

"Hey, Kev! Over here!"

His friend came running back from the loading dock zone. The news of Pamela's activity upset Kevin just as much as it had Thor.

"Why did she take a solo mission?" he yelled, kicking the ground. "What are we going to do about the professor?"

"I don't know, but we need to give him the details about that scrap yard. He's the only one who can do anything."

"Where is he?"

They looked over to the main office complex. More trucks, each with the triple white pyramid design and unknown cargo, headed past toward the exit.

"Oh, no. Trouble," murmured Kevin.

Walking toward them were Ray Ginsler and Douglas Mills. The project supervisor was clutching a roll of drafting paper held like a baseball bat.

"Put on a happy," whispered Thor.

The men continued walking and indicated that the boys should follow alongside.

"Professor Coleman won't be able to join you now," Ginsler told them. "He still has a number of adjustments to complete. There's a deadline to meet. Everyone is on double shifts."

"When will he be available?"

Their pace quickened. Ginsler was trying to shake the boys off. "Tomorrow. Maybe sometime in the afternoon."

"Thanks," said Thor.

The youths changed direction and headed for the parking lot.

"Hey!" yelled Mills after them. "Where's your sister?"

"She's . . ."

"Waiting in the car!" Thor completed Kevin's sentence.

Their response satisfied Mills. He ran to catch up with Ginsler at the reactor tower loading dock.

The boys broke into a run, making a beeline for their car.

A Geiger Scanner reading of +.08 rems indicates Danger if Exposed for More than Three Hours. Pamela Powell had entered the second hour of her journey.

The tractor-trailer was built for heavy loads, but its shock absorbers were long gone. Radiation was not the only danger to Pam. Just as menacing were the shifting stacks of sealed barrels. Every bump in the road brought another one crashing down.

Her eyes had became accustomed to the darkness. The hum through her earphone relayed data from the Geiger Scanner. The transmission pulse of the homing beacon remained constant. She sensed that the boys were tuning in.

The minutes passed slowly by. Pamela took a small plastic container from her purse and swallowed another yellow capsule of potassium iodide B-3.

The brakes squealed suddenly as the truck ground to a halt, sending more barrels loose. The voices of the two men from the driver's cabin moved along the side of the trailer and around to the rear.

Pamela felt her stomach turn queasy. Her hiding place was about to be exposed.

The rear loading door was raised, and sunlight broke through the dark interior. The girl was helpless.

"Why didn't you notify me?" screamed Ginsler.

The bald technician remained silent.

"When did this come in?" the project supervisor continued to shout.

"Late last night," the tall technician reported. "We kept it in the bag, sir, and sent in the report."

"Mills! Where's the report? Why didn't I get it?"

Douglas Mills shrugged nervously. "There's a chance Coleman received it. He was working all night, Ray. You gave him the hijacked shipping claims to verify."

"That old buzzard!" cursed Ginsler. "If this gets any further . . ."

"It won't," promised the bald technician.

"It better not, or your bodies will end up in this bag!" raved the man.

The lead-lined sack containing evidence of the security breach rested on the side of the loading dock. Ray Ginsler had heard that Public Health Officials had examined its contents and found traces of radioactive fission chips.

"Take care of Coleman," he ordered Mills.

Ginsler knew that the shoes encrusted in radioactive muck were not those of adults.

"And Mills! Get those kids!"

# CHAPTER 10

# Places in the Databases

The rear trailer door slammed shut again and darkness cloaked the stuffy interior once more. A hand groped from underneath paper tubes. Pamela Powell pulled herself up from her hiding place behind a mound of cylinder casings.

"I knew they'd be good for something," she managed to smile.

If the casings had not been piled up to stop the barrels from sliding, she would certainly have been discovered. Still, she remained a prisoner as the ride resumed.

The first thing she noticed was silence from the Geiger Scanner. Pamela recalled what she had overheard during the last stop.

"When are the fuel bundles coming?" asked one man.

"The next load. Take this for now," said another.

"Fine. Drop it off and we'll send it down to the lab," stated a third voice.

Then she had heard grinding on the floor as the men hoisted out the cargo container. Pam remembered holding on tightly to the cylinder casings. Only when the door closed did the thumping of her heart return to normal. It was then that she noted the Scanner's silence. Whatever the men had unloaded contained nuclear waste!

"The scrap metal yard!" Thor concluded.

"But she's not there," reported Kevin.

The homing beacon radar indicated Pamela was in transit again. On the dashboard, the radar's miniscreen displayed the signal from the girl's transmitter. The beacon registered the delays in every location where she stopped longer than three minutes. Two points at the scrap metal yard still glowed on the screen.

"We just missed her," Thor told his friend. "Seems she's on the expressway now."

He pressed a switch beside the radar. Its Rangefinder system kicked into action. A locator pinned down the exact presence of the blip.

"Guess where it's heading?"

"Where?" Kevin asked impatiently.

"Stanton."

The super turbocharger roared under the hood as the sports car veered into the express lane.

"Keep your eyes open," Kevin said from the side of his mouth.

The RearVu screen displayed an open road behind them. This diminished in a blur as they rocketed along the expressway. Thor handed a piece of gum to Kevin, then took three pieces for himself.

"How about the C.R?"

Thor acted on the suggestion. He picked up the microphone of the cellular radio and dialed his parents' call code. Despite a few attempts, there was no response.

"They must be out. What about Sergeant Dalby?"

Thor hesitated. "What can we tell the police, Kev? We don't know exactly who Pam is with. She may have gotten a lift back to town. Besides, how can we say what type of car she's in?"

"I'm counting on that!" Kevin snapped, pointing to the homing beacon radar screen.

The target circle displayed the transmitter's precise location. The youths saw themselves drawing closer. Every mile closed the gap.

"If I get through this, I could join the circus as an acrobat," thought Pamela as she gritted her teeth.

Sharp turns were becoming more frequent. Holding on to the teetering barrels and keeping her balance in the darkness required agile moves. Looking on the bright side of her predicament, she thought that the noises outside indicated the tractor-trailer was in a city. Car horns were blaring, and the stop-and-go shifts reminded her of driving with Kevin. For once, that thought gave her comfort.

"Maybe I should try to pull up that door. In city traffic someone would see me," she considered. But a cautionary thought followed. "They probably have an escort car behind this. Or another truck."

The brakes screeched again. Three barrels crashed to the floor. Darkness made the noise more terrifying. The tractor-trailer was turning in a wide circle. Finally, it came to a stop. She heard the driver's door closing and footsteps coming around to the rear door.

"Oh, no!" She held her breath.

Then the driver's footsteps became fainter. Was he walking away from the rig?

The girl stood up and listened intently. She heard a car pull up on the other side. It stopped, but remained idling.

"Aaaahhh," she breathed fearfully.

Scratching sounds came from the rear. Somebody was trying to break in!

"The hijackers!" she gasped.

The metallic sounds tore through her mind. What would hijackers do with her? She might have been able to stall the Emerald driver with excuses. But hijackers? They were real criminals! To them, a stowaway meant a police witness!

Suddenly, the lock broke free. The door flew upwards and the afternoon sunlight poured into the stuffy cargo hold.

"Pamela?"

Kevin's voice startled the prone figure. Pam moved a cylinder casing cautiously aside and peeked out.

"Kevin!"

He said nothing, but waved her to hurry out. He continued looking over his shoulder as Pamela jumped down from the trailer.

They were stopped in a city parking lot. The driver had gone into a nearby restaurant and Thor was keeping watch. Kevin lowered the trailer door and clamped the lock tight.

"You're lucky it wasn't sealed."

"And that my solar cell works," she told him, touching the homing transmitter.

Thor rushed over to the couple. "The driver's coming back!"

Just as Pam slid into the rear seat of Kevin's car, Thor put out his hand.

"I've got an idea. Give me the homer!"

She unclasped the homing beacon. Thor took the wad of gum he had been chewing and squeezed the tiny transmitter device into the gooey mess. He dashed to the tractor-trailer and stuck the wad under the cabin.

"Okay!" he shouted, leaping back into the sports car.

Pamela looked back from her seat at the vehicle that had been her prison for the last two hours. The unaware driver came back out as the MicroKidz sped off.

"How long were you following me?"

"You mean racing you! He's a crazy driver."

Thor agreed. "We've had you on the radar since you left the scrap metal yard."

"But I wasn't there."

"According to this homing detector, you sure were," he told her.

"But that's impossible!"

"Why?" asked Kevin.

"Because if I went there, this Geiger Scanner would have blown itself to bits!"

While Kevin tried keeping his eyes on the road, he motioned to Thor for an explanation. The youth was already turned and listening to Pam.

"There was a small container of radioactive material on board. I know, because it registered +8 rems. But it was unloaded. After that, the Scanner was silent," she declared with certainty. "You know what the radiation level was earlier at the scrap yard, Kevin. We couldn't even go down that laneway. No, they must have driven to another place."

Thor contemplated her facts. "No radioactivity at that stop?"

"The only hot item was that container."

Kevin considered the same possibilities as his friend.

"Pam, we drove by that laneway. The target circle intersected right at that point," he explained. "This homing beacon was aligned last week. It's 150 percent accurate!"

Thor picked up on that. "Since you weren't able to see the place they stopped, you don't know for certain. You're going on what the Scanner should have done if you went there, right? Two things might have happened. First, the power source in the Scanner is bonkers."

Pamela protested at once. "Look. The battery light is positive!"

"Or second, all the radioactivity was removed from around the scrap metal yard."

The mystery deepened. Rendering an area safe after exposure to high levels like that? Such a process was unknown. If this was the case, a new scientific discovery had been established.

"Where are we going?" asked Pam.

"To the workshop," said Thor, as Kevin spun onto the Cartesian Freeway.

"Stop by the Public Health Center. Dr. Skyne should know about this right away!"

Thor asked for her patience. "We'll go there after. First, we have a disk from the OptoScope to process."

It was late afternoon by the time Kevin parked in his driveway and the trio climbed out.

"I have to clean up," Pam said, stepping onto the side porch. The journey inside the trailer had left her clothes dusty and oily. She wanted a relaxing shower and some food.

The boys headed for the workshop behind the Bensons' garage. Kevin tapped his friend on the shoulder. It was a reminder to avoid trouble.

"Thanks, Kev. Almost forgot."

The youngster reached behind the garage drainpipe and released the hidden deactivator switch. Had Thor failed to press it, a secret alarm would have rung at Stanton Police headquarters. He already had a few false alarms to his credit; any more, and the responding officer would be obliged to issue a fine.

Mr. Chips's backup security program was also deactivated. The domestic robot stood silently guarding the lab as the boys began their work.

"When was the last time this was used?" Kevin asked in disgust.

Thor saw his friend holding a soggy plastic container. Liquid chemical sealer was dripping onto the floor.

"Hey, don't make a mess! Put it back!"

"I can't, Thor. This developing tank is filthy. How can I use it for the OptoScope disk? It hasn't been cleaned in months!"

"Then get yourself busy!"

There was tension between them now. In their race to reach conclusions they were becoming irritable. Each was afraid of making a mistake.

Kevin cleaned the disk-developing tank under a stream of ultrasonic waves. Then he emptied the OptoScope, loaded the disk in, and gave the timer full exposure.

Meanwhile, Thor had logged on to the federal databases through his RND microcomputer.

"Going to trace the License to Decommission," he mumbled.

"What good will that do?"

"Won't know until I see it."

He began the computer search with a standard inquiry. This was a legal search and it would leave a trail back to this outlet. Interceptors along the way would be able to contact him and unexpected information might be released.

In the Nuclear Regulatory Agency listing, the License to Decommission for Emerald had been administered to Raymond Ginsler. It did not surprise the youth that Douglas Mills had no listing.

"REQUEST : M1T1G5 : SCRAP METAL YARDS," Thor entered on the RND. He limited the search for entries to the area surrounding the yard's location.

"Nothing," he muttered at the blank screen.

Worn down by the frantic pace, Kevin sat nearby and let out a long sigh. While waiting for the OptoScope disk to be developed, he pulled out the computer analysis copy of the

Radiation Chamber tests. Kevin loaded Dr. Skyne's disk recording of the fission chips.

Images of subatomic forces exploded on the remote wall monitor. Kevin watched mesmerized, knowing they had originated in the muck that once clung to his shoes.

He looked over at Thor working on the computer.

"What would happen if you transmitted this data?"

Thor glanced up from the keyboard. "Why do that?"

"Just asking."

"I guess whoever received it would think whatever they were told. Like, the preceding instructions might tell them one thing, and then they see that coming . . . . ," Thor muttered, as he resumed working. "Don't know though."

Kevin's shoulders dropped in a tired shrug. As he watched the subatomic display, another exhausted yawn was released.

"Ooohhh . . . . Wrecked, man. I feel absolutely wrecked."

Thor's hands returned to the keyboard. Onto the RND micro monitor he typed, "REQUEST : MITIG5 : AUTO WRECK-ERS." He then entered the previous location estimate.

The RND hummed through the federal databases.

Three entries returned. The middle listing read "TRIPLE PYRAMIDS AUTO WRECKERS."

"Thanks, Kevin."

"For what?" he muttered.

He didn't get up to see the Triple Pyramids owner's name flash on the screen : "DOUGLAS MILLS."

# CHAPTER 11
# Load-and-Go

"Mills! Down here!"

Ray Ginsler's amplified voice resounded across the scrap metal yard. Three tractor-trailers were backed under the huge open shelter. Douglas Mills was standing on the roof.

"Checking the transfer valves!" he shouted.

"Get down before you go with it!"

Mills crept toward a ladder on the side. He grasped it and descended. Over his shoulder, he saw two men wearing silver antiradiation outfits. Only their eyes were visible through reinforced plexiglass visors. The drivers in each of the vehicles were similarly dressed.

Above the yard's office, the triple pyramid design caught the sun's glare. Its reflection fell on the dried path Doug Mills used to reach the shed. As he entered, Ginsler spoke into the microphone again.

"Start Procedure One."

Douglas Mills stood alongside his partner as they observed the activity through a safety-glass window. The tractor-trailers' rear doors flew open. Their drivers emerged and assisted in transferring the loads.

An hour later, the job was completed. Three shipments had became one large order. Barrels, boxes, machine tools, cylinder casings, and bulk waste containers lay dumped nearby. The truck emptied of these scrap metal parts now groaned under the weight of newer supplies.

"What's the reading?"

Mills checked the meter on the office Geiger Scanner. He rotated the remote probe mounted on the roof.

"We're in the clear. + .14. Hardly any spillage."

"That's a change," commented Ginsler.

"Do you want to wait for the big load to settle? I'd recommend that before we synthesize."

"Is there enough time?"

Mills shrugged. "Not really."

Over the loudspeaker, Ginsler announced new orders.

"Crew to pumping unit. Both drivers of empty trailers, please continue on your route."

Two technicians in protective clothing directed those vehicles forward. Once the trucks had left the shelter, the technicians moved toward an aluminum crate. Together they lifted it aside to reveal a pumping fixture partly buried in the ground.

"What's the delay?" Ginsler's voice boomed over the speaker.

The technicians pulled a thick metallic hose from the fixture up to the remaining tractor-trailer. Another hose was uncovered from an outlet hidden by a pillar. The driver drew back his side loading doors. Once inside, he opened four drums stamped Radioactive. Each technician placed his hose into the drum barrels. The driver then waved toward the office shed.

"Start it up," Ginsler signaled.

Mills started up the pumping system. A graph display in his briefcase microcomputer showed the rate of synthesis. They watched this final procedure, smiles increasing as the load capacity reached its limit.

"No further delays?" asked Ginsler.

His partner reassured him.

"Is the delivery coming up from the shaft?"

"Any minute," replied Mills.

In the center of the scrap metal yard, a pair of industrial robots rumbled out of a concrete shaft that resembled a vault entrance once used as an air-raid shelter. From this underground post, the industrial robots transported eight cylinder casings.

"Remote carriers approaching," Ginsler announced.

At his side, Mills directed the robots by remote control to approach the open shelter. They deposited the bulging cylinder casings inside the tractor-trailer, while the technicians stood back.

When the robots came out, they retraced their movements and returned to the concrete shaft.

The technicians completed the transfer and synthesis operation. They changed, showered, and took an ultrasonic cleaning in a smaller, adjacent shed. When they were ready, they reported to Ray Ginsler.

"Tank one is full to the max," reported the bald technician.

"You'll have to order a seal for the pumper, Ray," advised the taller man. "It's a leaker."

Ginsler took note of his suggestion while Mills conducted a final survey.

"Still steady," he said, checking the Geiger Scanner. "We should move out now."

The two technicians started for the door.

"Not you pair, not yet," Ray told them. "I want you back down in the lab."

The bald man protested. "We've done three transfers already!"

Ginsler nodded. "I know. A change in scheduling says

we could have another three tonight."

"What's the big rush?" demanded the tall technician.

"Nothing to worry about," smiled Mills. "Just prepare the shaft laboratory for a night shift."

He followed Ray out, leaving the two men behind. The driver of the lone tractor-trailer started his engine. Ginsler and Mills climbed into their car and escorted the truck down the tree-lined lane. At the end, where the roadway connected, they separated.

Ginsler and Mills turned in the direction of the Emerald Nuclear Generating Station. The hijacked truck, with its deadly cargo, continued its escape.


"What does that look like, Pam?"

"If you can't focus it, how can I tell?"

"That's as clear as it gets," explained Thor. "Your brother forgot to shoot through a filter."

"Hey, Benson, your finger pressed it loose!"

"Sure doesn't look like people there."

Though Pamela tried her best, she noted only blurred figures on the screen. The OptoScope disk required intense development and this had made the resulting image hard on the eyes.

"Try the image enhancer," she suggested.

"Believe it or not, this is it," Thor said patiently. "It's just not humanly possible to make it any clearer than this."

The girl studied the series of electronic photos taken from the laneway. She recalled the high radiation counts measured. Was the blurred image caused by that? Then Thor's words, "It's just not humanly possible...." came to mind. Why, of course it wasn't!

"You're both trying to detect human activity there, when all these moving figures are actually robots!"

The boys gave her puzzled looks.

"What else could function in an area so radiated? Those are robots carrying out remote-controlled orders! Take a closer look."

Her theory made what they were seeing more reasonable. Several small figures were moving oddly. Some held objects that humans would have to carry in different positions.

"What do you think they're working on?" Kevin wondered.

"One thing I'll bet they're *not* getting is spare parts from old cars!"

They all laughed at Pamela's remark.

The mystery of the scrap metal yard was put temporarily on hold while the trio prepared a fast meal. When he had switched the microwave oven on, Thor stepped into the hallway to check on the incoming message light flickering on the TeleMail link. Thor activated the printer. The message was from Professor Coleman: "HOPE YOU ARE FEELING BETTER, EDWARD. HAVE YOUR SON KEVIN AND HIS FRIEND THOR PAY A RETURN VISIT. BEST WISHES TO YOUR WIFE, ALAN."

Thor instantly recognized the professor's intention. By switching their names, he wanted to indicate to the boys that something was wrong.

While rushing through their meal, the MicroKidz reviewed the string of bizarre events. Professor Coleman's message was obviously a secret plea for help. The strange occurrences at the scrap metal yard hadn't been fully explained. And still, the hijacking of the trucks had to be sorted out.

"How are they all connected?" wondered Pam.

"Sometimes we never know enough until we know more than enough."

"Meaning that when you're in the middle of things, it's

tough to figure out relationships," added Thor. "But we'll keep working on it."

A scene of controlled scientific frenzy erupted. The workshop became their launching pad as they planned a journey into the unknown. They would leave nothing to chance.

"Let's start with the Data Disperser," Thor proposed.

This was their chance to utilize some of the outdated electronics gear from the Emerald Nuclear Generating Station. The MicroKidz liked the irony in their using the station's generating equipment to solve mysteries generated by the station.

"Cue it up to the disk drive through the patch," Thor instructed Kevin, who scrambled for the wires.

Eventually, they located the copy of the Public Health disk that had examined the fission chips. Kevin had filed it incorrectly, but Pam managed to root it out.

"When we preset this mode, the Data Disperser should shift into action," explained Thor. "The disk will feed itself through the Disperser."

No further details were necessary. The MicroKidz knew the plan. All they had to do was work together quickly and they would be successful.

"Bring on the star!" Pam finally said.

Mr. Chips was given a new program addition. Into the robot's microcircuitry, they implanted three remote control devices and a transmitter booster. But they ran into difficulty with the most important accessory, the Fission Tracer.

"Where do we put it?"

The crystalline case with the ruby-coated metal suited the robot as a hat. However, style was not a requirement, and they needed to connect it somehow.

"We might have to take off an arm," Kevin concluded. "The socket is a perfect place to bolt the Tracer. And the fibre-optic contacts are already there."

With a screwdriver and a laser-solder, Kevin had the Fission Tracer connected and the transmitter adjusted in twenty minutes. The unit was complete.

"A Radioactive Rover!" Pam labeled it.

Pam and Kevin carried Mr. Chips outside, where he began to operate on his own power, wheeling over to the Powells'.

Thor, meanwhile, left a message for his parents on their micro. Should they call through, it would let them know of his travel plans and expected return time. He hesitated sending any message to Sergeant Dalby until they knew for certain some crime had been committed.

Then they strapped a packing crate on the trunk of the sports car and settled Mr. Chips into his cosy space.

"If anybody makes fun of my driving, they can change places with Chips," Kevin joked.

Kevin pulled out slowly, taking extra care with his full load. Their first stop was the Public Health Inspection Center. Pamela wanted to update Dr. Skyne.

"I hope she won't be too upset that I'm taking another shift off. There's a few others who can fill in. Anyways, I am doing related work."

"Make it quick," Kevin told her as they parked in front of the building.

Thor watched her run inside. Kevin climbed out and checked the straps holding Mr. Chips to the luggage rack.

Moments later, Pamela came out of the Center. Her pale expression indicated something had gone wrong.

"They've left! Closed up everything!"

"Who's left?"

"Dr. Skyne! And Harry, too! Somebody said they were picked up by two men!"

The MicroKidz felt time sliding away as they wondered what had happened. Kevin raced the car onto the Cartesian Freeway.

The news on the radio was even more disturbing. " . . . . and the Highway Patrol reports that three transport trucks have been hijacked. Reports indicate that the stolen cargo is of a dangerous nature, although police will not specify . . ."

"They don't want to cause panic by telling people there's a possibility of a nuclear waste spill on the highway," Thor said.

" . . . . and if you have any information, contact the police headquarters nearest you. In other news . . . . " the announcer's voice faded as Kevin switched off the radio.

On the corner of the dashboard, Thor tapped the homing beacon receiver to activate the element. He tried scanning the rader, yet each time he adjusted it the target circle returned to 00/00.

"What are you trying to tune in?" asked Kevin.

"That transmitter I stuck in the gum. You know, onto that truck we got Pam from."

He played with the radar screen and tuner. The target circle still remained at 00/00. Dead center.

"When was this thing aligned?"

"I told you, last week," Kevin said, concentrating on the road ahead. "It's working perfectly."

"No it isn't. Every time I adjust it, the circle comes back to the middle."

Suddenly, Thor and Pamela saw Kevin staring into the RearVu screen with a look of horror on his face. They both turned and discovered why the homing beacon radar insisted on Dead Center.

The tractor-trailer was bearing down on them from behind at full speed!

## CHAPTER 12

# Stringing a Line Driver

Headlights flashed. Air horns screamed a warning. The grille of the tractor-trailer covered the entire rear window view!

"Pull over!" Pamela cried out.

A car blocked them on the right side, a concrete divider rose on the left. Their only chance for escape was straight ahead.

"Hang tight!" yelled Kevin.

He flipped on the super turbocharger. The car almost lifted off the expressway, surging forward in flight. When a space opened up in the other lane, Kevin veered in and cut the turbocharger. A gust of wind swept by as the tractor-trailer flew past. Triple white pyramid mudflaps verified its identity.

"What's his rush?"

"Maybe he's carrying a full load," Kevin answered his sister, "or trying to outrun someone who's after it."

"Or it could just have been hijacked," added Thor. "Why don't you follow it?"

"What for?"

Kevin tapped the radar to show that physical pursuit was

unnecessary. The homing beacon screen read out the exact location of the truck carrying its transmitter.

"Are you happy with the results?"

"Of what?"

"The beacon. You said it wasn't accurate."

"I take it all back, Kevin."

They continued on, following the highway traffic that seemed to move endlessly, connecting small towns and villages to larger centers.

Soon, they pulled onto an exit ramp that led out onto a country road. In the distance, they could see the line of trees running down the laneway to the scrap metal yard. As they neared the showdown, final plans were settled.

"Start with these, just in case," Pam said.

She took out three potassium iodide B-3 capsules to swallow so they would not be endangered if a sudden rise in the radiation level were to occur. The pills, however, were no protection against other forms of assault.

They stopped at the end of the laneway. There was no apparent activity. With the probe of her Geiger Scanner, Pam checked the zone ahead.

"All clear," she said, slightly amazed. "I don't know how they do it."

"We'll find out," Thor promised.

Kevin scanned the yard area with the OptoScope. He checked each section closely, looking out for the big robots. When he gave the sign, they unloaded Mr. Chips.

"Pull his eye out," instructed Thor.

Kevin unwound a lens cap from the top section of the robot and withdrew an implanted video lens. Meanwhile, Thor adjusted his RearVu screen on the dashboard.

"It's clearing through."

The images Mr. Chips recorded through his lens appeared on the mini-screen. Using remote control, the robot would be sent on a tour while the youngsters observed from their safe position. Because they feared unknown radioactive leaks, Mr. Chips became their on-site representative.

"Don't get into any trouble," said Pam as she checked the Fission Tracer and secured it tighter in the arm socket.

They watched the robot wheel down the laneway at top speed. As it passed a familiar area, Thor laughed at the Vu screen display. The steel cable they'd used to pull the professor's car free was lying between two trees.

"Still there," he chuckled.

"Sure, ready for next time."

The metallic rover moved like an intruder from another planet. Its remote-controlled video eye scanned the surroundings: the trees, the fields, the fences, the rusted autos.

"What's that?" asked Kevin.

The Vu screen showed two moving forms shifting about in an irregular manner. A zoom shot clearly identified them.

"Industrial robots," noted Pamela.

The large robots were transporting bulging cylinder casings to a concrete portal. The open portion of this shaft seemed to be the entrance for an underground vault. After a few minutes, the pair of robots emerged for another load.

Mr. Chips remained stationary. Its electronic lens followed the action as the other robots moved under the transfer shelter. Three additional robots were there, lifting and sorting more casings. Two were manipulating barrels labeled Radioactive Waste. These were also transported into the concrete shaft.

"What's registering?" asked Thor.

Pam glanced at her Geiger Scanner. "Nothing."

"Can we try a pan around the yard?"

Kevin pointed to the Vu screen. "You saw those barrels. And you know what's in those cylinders, right? That's why only robots are on the site!"

To satisfy them, Kevin maneuvered the remote controller. At the same time, Thor tuned in the mobile cellular radio. Sounds picked up by Mr. Chips's microphone came through the car speaker.

"Engine noise. Machine noise," Kevin reported.

The microphone captured the sounds of the robots at work. However, a different tone came over the speaker too.

"Voices!" breathed Pamela.

"Find out where they're coming from," said Thor.

Kevin sent their remote-controlled robot into another circuit. It spun slowly in a circle until the audio directional finder located the source of the voices. On the Vu screen, the youngsters saw the yard's office shed.

Now, Kevin directed Mr. Chips toward the building, but steered it around to the side, away from the door. He stopped the robot beside the wall and extended a microphone prod from the unit to touch the metal siding. This brought a clear recording of audio signals back to the car speaker.

"When do you go?"

"If we don't get a call soon, I'm leaving."

"I'll be right behind you."

The MicroKidz instantly recognized the voices of the two odd technicians who worked at Emerald.

"What does Ray want from Coleman?"

"A guarantee," replied the other. "He'll set the professor free if the old man promises to keep his mouth shut."

"Think he'll refuse?"

"Only if he wants to die."

Those words chilled the listeners in the sports car.

"He's really in trouble," Pamela breathed.

"That explains his strange message to us," said Thor. "He was probably under guard when he sent the TeleMail notice. The only way to warn us was by switching our names."

The speaker crackled again. The technicians were heard moving around in the office shed.

"Everything okay outside?"

"A-OK. Robotics on schedule."

A new image appeared now through Mr. Chips's electronic lens. An industrial robot, carrying a thick cylinder casing, came into view. Thor tapped Kevin's shoulder.

"Follow that one!"

The microphone prod was retracted, and the little robot went into forward gear, chasing the larger model. The pair were soon side by side.

"How far do you want me to go?"

"Stay right with it," Thor said briskly.

They had a clear image of Mr. Chips's journey on the Vu screen. He seemed to be escorting the worker robot to the entrance of the concrete shaft.

"Should I send him in?"

Kevin got the go-ahead. The image was so clear, and the tension so high, that it felt as if they were going into the tunnel themselves.

The rovers entered the dark concrete shaft. Mr. Chips's infrared filter brought light to the darkness in the interior of the narrow, descending structure.

"This might have been a mine shaft once," observed Pamela.

"Could be. See those rails on the side?"

Kevin steered Mr. Chips out of the path of an oncoming robot returning for another load.

"Looks like the bottom here," reported Kevin, pointing to the lower part of the screen where a mound of used cylinder casings lay stacked. The robot accompanying Mr. Chips placed its full casing on the ground, swung around, and began its ascent to the surface.

"Check out this place."

The electronic lens scanned the shaft interior.

Suddenly, before their eyes, a crack in the rock wall widened to reveal a human figure wearing a silver antiradiation suit!

The youngsters were stunned. They watched the mysterious figure walk over to the casing, lift it very carefully, and return with it to the opening in the wall. He stepped in and the door closed automatically behind him.

"Start the Fission Tracer!" ordered Thor.

Kevin rotated the arm socket control. The mechanism deployed. They watched Mr. Chips attach the Fission Tracer against the door of the room. Slowly, its ruby-coated metal began to react and emit a pulse throughout the unit.

"According to the Fission Tracer, they're running a steady stream of radioactive particles in there," Thor concluded.

"That must be a lab inside!" added Kevin.

The youngsters realized the great danger beyond that door.

"Get Chips out of there," said Thor.

Kevin gave the controls to Pamela who directed their robot's ascent to the surface. With a tug on Thor's arm, he pulled him up the laneway.

"What are you doing? We're not going to that shed, Kevin!"

"We have to protect ourselves!"

He led Thor to the spot where the professor's car had

been stuck. Kevin hauled out the heavy gauge steel cable.

"Give me a hand."

Together, they strung the cable across the laneway. Suspended at knee level between two trees, the cable became a near-invisible barrier across the road. Then they returned to the car.

"How is he doing?"

"Almost out," Pam replied.

The Vu screen showed the area in front of the robot becoming brighter. Pam shut off the infrared filter. But just as Mr. Chips rolled out of the shaftway, two unexpected figures came into view. The two technicians were waiting!

Their voices broke through the cellular radio speaker.

"Get that thing! Hold it back!"

"I'll do better!"

The bald technician knocked the robot over with a powerful kick. A foot was the final image the MicroKidz saw on the screen before transmission stopped.

"Fast! Out of here!"

Kevin scrambled into the driver's seat at the same time as Thor and Pam squeezed in the other side. The sports car screeched around in a full circle. Stones and dirt flew up as the wheels spun harder for traction. With the steering column pressed tight, Kevin raced down the long, narrow laneway. Trees flashed by on each side. Thor's arm comforted Pam over the sudden bumps.

"Oh no!" they shouted together.

A tractor-trailer was heading down the laneway towards them and there wasn't room to pass!

"Only one chance," muttered Kevin.

He braked the vehicle while spinning the wheel and the car skidded around. Halfway through the turn he accelerated. They were now speeding away from the tractor-trailer.

"Kevin! You can't go anywhere!"

Thor's warning reminded Kevin about the steel cable they had put up across the lane. They had set it up to save themselves but now they were trapped.

Reluctantly, Kevin brought the car to a halt. Thor, however, was not giving up. He reached for the cellular radio and began tuning in to the police frequency.

"Get out now!" a man's voice yelled.

Before he could send a message, Thor was dragged from the car. The tractor-trailer had stopped right behind them. The hulking driver held on to Thor and Pamela, and Douglas Mills grabbed Kevin. He smashed the boy with his fist. Kevin let out a scream.

"You kids have had it! And not just for trespassing!"

As the MicroKidz shivered helplessly, they saw a pickup truck racing down the laneway towards them.

"Stop them!" screamed Thor.

The driver mistook his warning for a threat. He drove a fist into Thor's stomach, crumpling the boy in pain.

An astonishing scene followed, as events unfolded in an unreal, almost slow-motion, sequence. The pickup truck was speeding closer. Suddenly, as the steel cable barrier dug in under the wheels and front bumpers, two trees on each side of the road snapped from the force, and the pickup truck was torn in half! The wheels and chassis froze to a halt. The cabin, however, continued to sail through the air, its startled passengers in flight without a plane. It crash-landed fifty feet away.

## CHAPTER 13
# Deadly Fallout

The wire handcuffs were painful on the wrists of the MicroKidz.

They were standing against the wall of Ray Ginsler's office. Hands bound in front, the wire almost slicing into their skin, they felt defeated and afraid.

The project supervisor was speaking quietly on his private telephone, occasionally glancing over at the three youths. Nearby, Douglas Mills cradled a submachine gun on his lap.

"When are they going in?" Ginsler asked over the phone. "They're that bad? Will the emergency room be free after that?" He looked directly at Kevin. "Because there might be more 'accident' victims."

The youngsters shuddered. Ginsler was speaking to a hospital aide. He had learned that his two technicians were on their way to surgery.

"And you know what that means?" snarled the man.

No one dared reply.

"Let's drop them off the tower," snickered Mills.

"Not a bad idea."

"I think we'll call it a day," said Ginsler. "What do you say, Doug? Ready for an alert?"

He started toward a corner cabinet.

"No," protested Mills, pointing at the trio. "Not while they're here."

"They won't be much longer."

He pulled back the cabinet to disclose a secret control panel. A latch key was inserted and turned, and two buttons pressed.

Boom! Boom! Two deafening claps of thunder filled the sky.

The youngsters were astonished. So this was how the cloudless storms had occurred! Again, although there were no clouds in the sky, the thunder sounded as real as if a storm was imminent.

Another thunderous wave boomed over the Emerald Nuclear Generating Station and alarms discharged.

Ray Ginsler saw the frightened expressions on the youngsters' faces.

"Yes, all created from here. Electromagnetic discharges into the atmosphere are just one of our developments. You see, we're finding many uses for these fission byproducts. Most scientists, like your dear Professor Coleman, consider the dismantlement of nuclear reactors as the end of the line. Not so. In fact, I believe these misnamed 'waste' products are the most important part of the development. Fantastic for weapons!"

Another thunderclap roared out, as if in agreement. The office window rattled in the shock wave.

"This nuclear station is more valuable dismantled than when it was operating. And now, *I* say where the power goes!"

The pressure was too much for Pamela. She began to cry.

Thor and Kevin were too bewildered to be able to comfort her.

The alarms continued to sound. The work crews outside hurried to flee in buses and cars.

"Effective method of crowd control," Ginsler smiled. He waved at Mills. "Put them away."

Handcuffed and powerless, the trio was led out of the office. The hallways were deserted. Mills squeezed them into a service elevator and pressed a button with the tip of his gun.

"Where are we going?" Thor managed to ask.

"We like to surprise special guests," sneered Mills.

When they reached the basement, Mills gestured with his gun toward a corner door. He punched a digital wall lock to open the partition, and the trio stepped into a windowless room.

Sitting silently in the small room were Professor Coleman, Dr. Skyne, and Harry. They leaped up when the saw the new arrivals. Mills slammed the door on the prisoners and left.

"Here, let's get these off," Dr. Skyne said.

While she carefully unwound the wire handcuffs, they exchanged sombre greetings. Then they began to bring each other up-to-date on their experiences.

"Don't worry about speaking too loudly, because other people need to hear," shouted Professor Coleman. He pointed to the parabolic microphone mounted in the ceiling.

Dr. Skyne reported that she and Harry had been apprehended by the technicians who had carried away the radioactive soil samples. She wondered why, since they already had that material, as well as the computer analysis disk.

"Maybe they want me to work on something," she worried.

Harry, normally chatty and outspoken, was sitting silently at the edge of the group, staring at the floor.

Professor Coleman tried to boost their spirits by injecting some humor. The youngsters noticed that his face brightened each time he spoke with Dr. Skyne. Though a decade apart in ages, these two unmarried professionals seemed to share an understanding beyond the sciences.

"What's it like outside?" he asked. "I forget, having been stuffed in here all day."

"Not too bad," Kevin replied. "Except for the phony thunder."

"So you managed to see the man from Oz play his thunder machine?" the professor chortled loudly in the direction of the microphone.

"A little game of his to clear the air."

"And test low-level explosions in the atmosphere," added Dr. Skyne. She turned to the youngsters. "The professor and I have been comparing notes for the last few hours. We've concluded that Mr. Ginsler has developed some extraordinary uses for nuclear waste materials. He has the ability to decontaminate an area in a very short period of time."

"We found that out at the scrapyard," Thor told her. "In the morning the place was deadly, but a few hours later it was all clear."

"They have an underground lab, too," added Kevin, "at the bottom of a concrete mine shaft."

"Where is this place?" asked the professor.

Kevin described the location of the scrapyard in relation to the nuclear plant.

"Precisely the kind of place needed to launch particle

streams into the atmosphere! A deserted landscape, a junkyard used as a front to keep the authorities away. And, no doubt that lab is where they transfer and synthesize the waste."

They seemed to have unraveled the mystery. But what good was it if they were unable to get this information out? What would Ray Ginsler and Mills attempt next? What if a group of terrorists or an enemy power wanted this secret process? Was Ginsler controlling a potential Doomsday weapon?

Thor realized the time had come to put his plan into action.

"Mr. Ginsler? Hey! Ray!" he shouted directly underneath the microphone. "I know you're listening. So listen good! There's a transmission coming out over all Data-Link services! Hear that?"

The other captives watched the confident boy continue to yell at the ceiling microphone. Only Kevin and Pamela were aware that, in a short while, the Data Disperser in his garage workshop was scheduled to turn itself on for a national broadcast.

"Now, it's all automatic, preset and registered. At the end of the transmission, your name — and Mills's too — are given, as well as this location. It also says something about what you're up to! If you want to stop it before the broadcast gets to that point, then let me out! Just me! Alone!" His voice echoed back at him. He hoped his message was getting through. "Tune it in, Ray. DataLink 87-G7. You'll recognize the pictures."

Professor Coleman looked in amazement at the youth. Dr. Skyne came over and gave him a hug.

"I just hope you know what you're doing," she whispered.

So did Thor. This might be their one chance for escape.

He recalled a favorite saying of his: "When the going gets tough, the tough get going."

Twenty minutes later, the chamber door swung open. Douglas Mills stood in front of the prisoners, his submachine gun guaranteeing control. With a shake of the weapon, Mills indicated that Thor was to step out.

Thor watched the digital lock close behind him, but could not decipher the numbers. They left the basement stronghold by elevator. Not a word was exchanged.

Ray Ginsler stood by his office window, surveying the desolate scene outside. The twin reactor towers loomed before him. The work crew had left and everything was going ahead on schedule. No teenager was going to upset his plans.

"Wait in the hall," he told Mills, before turning to Thor.

"Well," Ginsler said flatly, "there's your show."

He pointed to his desktop display monitor. This monitor, and thousands of others around the country, were receiving the Public Health computer analysis disk. Thor kept his pleasure to himself. The Data Disperser was performing as programmed. He had to capitalize on that.

"Like I said downstairs, Mr. Ginsler. You see, I really did put it on DataLink. And at the end, your name and real business is announced."

The man crumpled a paper cup. "What do you want?"

"My friends set free."

"No! The professor and the doctor are too useful to me. As scientists and as hostages!"

"I meant Kevin and Pamela."

Ginsler laughed gruffly. "Is that all?" The kids were no threat to him. He pressed the intercom and Mills entered. "The other boy and girl. Get them! But leave the others!"

When his partner had left, Ray pointed to the DataLink reception. Thor resisted the order. He wanted his friends to be present before he intercepted the transmission at source.

Ginsler tensed up. "I don't know how you've managed to send this around the country, sonny. But if we get to the end, and my name and plans are mentioned, you and your friends are dead!"

The door swung open. Pam and Kevin were pushed inside. Mills followed, his submachine gun still trained on them.

"Now!" screamed Ginsler. "Cut into that link!"

Thor remained calm. His look at Kevin and Pamela prepared them both for action. He crossed in front of Mills to approach the office computer.

Ginsler started yelling again.

"Move it! Hurry up!"

As Thor entered his password onto the keyboard, he felt the icy steel gun barrel touch his back. It was time to act. He yelled, "Crashers!" and spun around in time to see Kevin kick the submachine gun loose!

Thor had tackled Mills before the weapon hit the floor. The man's head smashed onto the edge of a cabinet and he slumped unconscious to the floor.

Pamela struck Ray Ginsler across the chest with a cylinder casing before fleeing. It took the man a long moment to react and, in that time, the two boys had a chance to leap free. They slammed through the private passageway outside.

Ginsler examined his wounded partner. Blood was seeping from the back of Mills's head. Ginsler grabbed the submachine gun and gave chase.

The grounds were deserted. The eerie stillness that had fallen over the Emerald Nuclear Generating Station was broken now by shots fired into the air.

A falling brick from one of the partially dismantled

reactor towers alerted Ginsler to the boys' whereabouts. He moved into a better position to shoot.

"Get back here! Or I'm going into the basement to clean up!"

A piece of metal thrown from above narrowly missed him. Ginsler squinted. He knew exactly where they were hiding; inside the top rim of the reactor tower. And there, he had them trapped!

Ginsler scrambled to the crew platform used to mount the tower. The boys dropped more bricks and stones as the platform rose up the exterior wall. However, a metal sheet above the platform deflected the debris.

The scene at the top of the tower resembled the ruins of a Roman coliseum. The partially dismantled reactor tower was a huge, hollow structure. Portions of smashed concrete blocks and twisted steel rods dotted the crumbling rim. And beyond the rim, there was a two-hundred-foot drop!

"This is it! You can't get away! Everything's covered!" Ginsler's shout echoed in the ruins. "Come out now and I'll spare the others!"

Suddenly, a tremendous thunderclap boomed! The rim of the reactor tower shook. Loose rocks slid off the ledge.

From their hole in the side wall, Thor and Kevin felt the structure shake as if an earthquake had passed. They saw their chances of escape dwindling.

Slowly, they became aware of a distant, steadily increasing sound approaching.

Sirens!

Ray Ginsler stood up on the rim of the tower. Helplessly, he looked down on the advancing squad of police and military cars. With their sirens blaring, they smashed through the locked fences.

In a final frantic outburst, Ginsler began shooting at the

policemen. They did not get to return his fire. Another powerful thunderclap shook the tower and Ginsler lost his balance. He tripped over crumbling rocks and fell. His dying scream echoed up to the youths as his falling body was swallowed up inside the reactor tower.

## CHAPTER 14

# Fish and (Mr.) Chips

A police investigation declared the death accidental. Douglas Mills had suffered a concussion, but was out of danger. Along with the two technicians whose pickup truck was sheared on the laneway, he had a number of criminal and civil offences filed against him. They all recuperated in the same hospital ward, guarded around the clock by detectives.

For the MicroKidz, things were back to normal. The national media knew nothing of their adventure because of pressure from the federal government. Thor, Kevin, and Pamela had received a special visit from a highly placed federal official. The public was not to know how close they had come to a major tragedy. They also understood his request for a media blackout for purposes of national security.

But to each other, and to those who'd been involved, they were heroes. So, Mr. Benson organized a private celebration.

"The Big Byte? All right!"

Kevin's shout carried down Matrix Boulevard. His mother and sister came out of the house for the ride into town. The Benson family had left a few minutes earlier.

Kevin told them to hurry. "Let's get moving or there won't be any food left!"

"With you still here, there's no chance of that," answered Mrs. Powell.

They climbed into his sports car and drove off. Since his mother was in the passenger seat, Kevin was the perfect example of a courteous driver. Mrs. Powell, of course, was not fooled.

The lights at the Big Byte flashed brightly. Mr. Benson had rented the high-tech restaurant for the evening, and everyone was in a holiday mood.

When the Powell family entered, the celebration was already in full swing. Trays of tasty snacks and frothy fruit drinks were passed around. Music pumped from the speakers on each table as the video screens displayed pop performers in concert.

Professor Coleman and Dr. Skyne were engaged in a lively discussion. Harry, it seemed, shared a common trait with Kevin: they both had enormous appetites. Sergeant Dalby was off duty and chatting with three people from BenDaCon. As well, a few teachers from Stanton High School had been invited by Mrs. Powell.

Thor sat at a side table with Pamela. They took their time sipping fruit drinks and chatting.

"What would have happened if you hadn't found that switch?"

"To cause the thunder?"

"Yeah, 'cause Kevin and I were goners up there."

"If I hadn't seen that hidden panel earlier," Pam almost whispered, "I guess we wouldn't be sitting here tonight."

They shared a moment of thoughtful silence. Then Pam brightened up and grinned at Thor.

"This is Saturday night. Remember?"

Slowly it came to him. "A party. Some girl in your class, right? I know I promised, but we can't go and leave Kevin here."

Pamela looked over his shoulder toward the door and waved at someone just coming in to join them.

"Thor, this is Cheryl Tasel."

He turned to meet a smiling girl of sixteen. He recognized her from school, though he had never spoken to her.

"Coming to my party later?"

Before he could answer, Pamela had led Cheryl across the room and introduced her to Kevin.

Meanwhile, Professor Coleman and Dr. Skyne approached Thor. The boy rose to shake hands and noticed that the two older people were now holding hands.

"I want to thank you for introducing us," said the professor.

"It was a really roundabout way, wasn't it?" Dr. Skyne laughed.

A flourish at the back interrupted their conversation. The cook for the Big Byte called for attention.

"We're launching a new special of the house tonight. And it's being served by your not-so-dumbwaiter!"

The doors of the kitchen opened. Mr. Chips came wheeling out, balancing a tray. It held the party food, prepared especially to honor the trio.

"What is it?" Kevin wondered.

Pamela lifted the covering. "Are you ready for it?"

"What?"

"Fish and chips!"

The celebrants groaned and laughed at the pun. Kevin, for once, had something on his mind other than dinner. Cheryl held his arm as they approached Thor.

"Didn't Pam invite you to a party tonight?" Kevin said to Thor. "Well, let's get hopping. Cheryl has to get back to her place before the other kids arrive!"

With eager smiles, the four youngsters left the adults at the Byte and slipped unnoticed out into the night.

The MicroKidz needed to celebrate and relax, for they would soon be involved in another adventure. They didn't know it now, but they would discover that the freedoms that microtechnology bring to society can be abused to undermine the very basis of democracy. This mysterious threat will unfold in *DATA SNATCHERS*.